Buying a Property in France

Thank you for buying one of our books. We hope you'll enjoy the book and that it will help you find your dream home in France.

We always try to ensure our books are up to date, but contact details seem to change so quickly that it can be very hard to keep up with them. If you do have any problems contacting any of the organisations listed at the back of the book please get in touch, and either we or the author will do what we can to help. If you do find correct contact details that differ from those in the book, please let us know so that we can put it right when we reprint.

Please do also give us your feedback so we can go on making books that you want to read. If there's anything you particularly liked about this book – or you have suggestions about how it could be improved in the future – email us on info@howtobooks.co.uk.

Good luck with finding your property and we hope you enjoy life in France.

The Publishers
www.howtobooks.co.uk

D1417106

If you want to know how . . .

Buy to Let in France
How to invest in French property for pleasure and profit

Going to Live in France
Your practical guide to living and working in France

Starting & Running a B&B in France
How to make money and enjoy a new lifestyle running your own chambres d'hôtes

Living & Working in Paris
Your first-hand introduction to this capital city

Retire Abroad
Your complete guide to a new life in the sun

howtobooks

Please send for a free copy of the latest catalogue to:

How To Books
3 Newtec Place, Magdalen Road
Oxford OX4 1RE, United Kingdom
email: info@howtobooks.co.uk
www.howtobooks.co.uk

The Daily Telegraph

Buying a Property in
France

*An insider guide to realising
your dream*

CLIVE KRISTEN

howtobooks

Published by How To Books Ltd,
3 Newtec Place, Magdalen Road,
Oxford OX4 1RE, United Kingdom.
Tel: (01865) 793806. Fax: (01865) 248780.
email: info@howtobooks.co.uk
http://www.howtobooks.co.uk

First edition 1993
Second edition 2002
Reprinted 2002 (three times)
Reprinted 2003
Fully revised and reprinted 2003
Reprinted 2004

British Library Cataloguing in Publication Data.
A catalogue record for this book is available from
the British Library.

Produced for How To Books by Deer Park Productions
Typeset by Kestrel Data, Exeter, Devon
Line drawings by Nicki Averill
Cover design by Baseline Arts Ltd, Oxford
Printed and bound by Cromwell Press Ltd, Trowbridge, Wiltshire

Contents

Preface   ix

1   Why France?   **1**
First thoughts   1
The British invasion   1
Lifestyle   2
To buy or not to buy?   9
Need to know   13
What choice is there?   16

2   Where and what to buy   **21**
The regions   21
Target pointers   22
The French motorway network   38
Flying to your destination   40
The railways   42
Price guidelines   43
Buying at auction   48
Garaging and parking   49

3   Renting a property and timeshare   **51**
Hotels and guest houses   51
Holiday letting   52
Long-term letting   55

	Instalment purchase	58
	Timeshare	59
4	**Settling in France**	**64**
	Initial documentation	64
	Managing the removal	66
	Pets	68
	Healthcare	69
	Healthcare for residents	72
	Safeguarding your pension	74
	Education	75
	Utilities	78
	The media	86
	Motoring	88
5	**Financial matters**	**96**
	Banking in France	96
	Taxation	101
	Wills and inheritance	112
	Marriage contract	118
	Mortgages and loans	119
	Insurance	124
6	**The purchase process**	**126**
	The French estate agent	126
	The UK estate agent	128
	The notaire	130
	Additional cost of purchase	134
	Company property purchase	136
7	**Building or buying a property under construction**	**137**
	Building land	137
	The cost of building	138
	The building contract	141

Doing it yourself 143
Buying a property under construction 146

8 Your property as a gîte business **151**
Gîtes and the law 153
Making a profit 156
A gîte as a business 159

9 Setting up a business in France **161**
The professional advisors 161
What kind of company? 164
Set up costs and formalities 167
Buying a commerial property 169
Leasing commercial property 170
Financing a business 173
Employing others 177
Communications 180
Setting up the business in the home 181

10 Business taxation and insurance in France **184**
The audit 184
Initial tax liability 185
Transfer duty (droits d'enregistrement) 186
Business licence tax (taxe professionelle) 186
Capital gains tax (taxe sur les plus values) 187
Corporation tax (impôts sur les sociétés) 188
Taxation of business income (impôt sur les
benefices industrielles et commerciaux) 189
Wages tax (taxes sur les salairies) 189
Value added tax (taxe sur la valeur ajoutée) 190
Branch profits tax 191
Supplementary flat rate taxation 192
Business insurance 192

11 The internet   **196**
   Buying a property   196
   Renting a property   198
   Financing the deal   199
   Managing your money   199
   Shopping   200
   Newspapers   201
   Radio   201

Further reading   202
Standard long-term letting contract   204
Index   211

Preface

Interest in French residential and commercial property has never been greater. Prices are lower than in the UK and the French climate and culture are powerful incentives to renters and buyers.

In this revision I have sought to improve and update straightforward, practical and independent advice on a broad range of related subjects, based on my own personal experience. This includes choices about buying and renting, the costs and intricacies of the legal processes, and how to avoid some of the pitfalls. Much has changed since our first edition in 1993, and even the new edition published in 2002. In addition to the updates the reader may now benefit from sections embracing the revised legislation, the internet and the euro.

As well as travel and holidays France offers a growing range of business opportunities. This may begin with a fact-finding mission, followed up by setting up an office or workshop. While other authors offer advice on domestic property few take account of more commercial considerations. It is hoped that this is remedied here.

I wish to express thanks to film producer, Bob Davis, for encouraging me to update the manuscript; to my wife Maureen, for helping me maintain the balance and flow of the revisions, and to Nickie Averill for the lovely illustrations.

Clive Kristen

1

Why France?

FIRST THOUGHTS

Around half an hour is all it takes on the swiftest routes to begin experiencing something very special. There are warm summer days and lazy evenings with good food and fine wine. There is the sound of the sea and the magic of the mountains. Here is a land of history and culture with quiet country roads and busy vibrant cities. There is something for everyone to enjoy in a country where children are made as welcome as their parents. The place is France: it is hardly surprising that it has become the UK's most popular holiday destination. Ten million Britons made the journey in 2002 and with more than 75 million visitors annually France is easily the most popular tourist destination in Europe.

THE BRITISH INVASION

It is not surprising that more and more Britons are becoming property owners on the other side of the channel. The idea is appealing for a number of reasons. France is our nearest neighbour, and most of us already have at least a smattering of the language. Life seems to run at an easier pace and the climate is generally better than our own. Since 1992 immigration has been easier, and the tunnel has fulfilled its promise of rapid, if rather expensive, transport. The Sea Cat, new super ferries and a network of regional airports make commuting a possibility, and modern communications means that many kinds of business can be run effectively from any base on Europe's mainland.

Perhaps the most obvious attraction is that property prices are well below our own. It may be true that there are fewer bargains to be had these days, especially in the most popular regions, but for those who live in the more expensive areas of the UK the difference remains quite staggering.

LIFESTYLE

The French lifystyle is very different to our own and there are great contrasts between city, suburban and rural areas. The overall population density is around one-third of that of the UK and nearly three-quarters of the people live in industralised urban areas. This means that French towns and cities are as busy, some would say busier, than our own.

Through vast expanses of countryside however the situation is reversed. The French call it *la vie tranquille* and it certainly is just that.

Visitors to France often form a mistaken impression of this

important difference between urban and rural life. Cities other than Paris may seem to be quieter than our own, and popular holiday resorts – especially on the coast – rather busier. This is because most visitors see France during July and August when the French themselves take their annual holidays.

The French have a high regard for intellect and education. They talk knowledgeably, even at cafe level, about nuances of debate in politics and religion. They are at the same time gregarious, yet dislike formal or organised activity. These apparent contradictions make the French what they are – elusive, infuriating, introverted, intriguing, beguiling and, most frequently, charming.

It is worth noting that when responding to questions about their motivation for buying property in France the British are inclined to list priorities such as cost, climate and cuisine. The British may receive a more positive response if they placed the French themselves towards the top of the list.

Climate

Climate is a factor overlooked at your peril if you intend to purchase property in France. It affects not only your own enjoyment of the property but its letting potential. France, as the largest country in western Europe, has considerable regional variations in climate.

We tend to think of France as being warmer and sunnier than Britain as it lies to the south. But this is not all together true: Calais, for instance, is more northernly, and colder and wetter than Plymouth.

Much of France lies in the northern temperate zone and is affected by the prevailing westerlies of the Atlantic. The Gulf Stream plays a significant part in determining the coastal climate. Brest in the north of Brittany enjoys similar winter temperatures to the Mediterranean resorts but is very much wetter and subject to fierce Atlantic gales. The climate to the northern and western regions of France is similar to that of Devon and Cornwall.

South of a line which roughly parallels the river Loire, the influence of the Mediterranean increases, and the climate is generally warmer and drier. The east of the country, towards the Alps, has a more typically European climate with a greater variation in seasonal temperatures. Both the Alps and the Pyrenees have climates that can be severe in winter and uncertain in summer. The Jura, it is alleged, has two seasons: summer, which lasts about six weeks, and winter. The central zone of France – influenced by the Massif – has the greatest temperature variation: Limoges, for instance, can vary up to 50°C over the course of the year (up to 35°C in August and down to –15°C for a few weeks during January and/or February). One compensation for these severe winters is that they are short.

| | January | | August | |
	Max.	Min.	Max.	Min.
Biarritz	12	6	24	16
Nantes	7	2	25	13
Nice	14	6	30	20
Paris	7	1	22	11

Figure 1. Average maximum and minimum temperatures.

It should be pointed out that regardless of climate variation the Alps is a special case. Because of skiing in the winter and general tourism in the summer, a 10-month season (normally excluding October and November) is possible and roads are kept open in a way which would seem almost unbelievable in the UK. The French are neither shocked nor surprised by accumulations of snow in hilly areas in the winter months.

Language

Largely through the influence of radio and television the French language has become more universal and standardised. There are still however, strong local variations, which reflect the history and traditions of the regions. The Bretons and Basques have languages of their own which are as fiercely preserved as the Welsh or Scottish Gallic tongues. There are, however, only a few isolated communities where the natives are not truly bilingual.

There is a range of dialect too. In Alsace, for instance, the Germanic influence remains strong. There are also measured regional dialects and different kinds of accents: the 'street language' of Paris and Marseille creates problems not only for the visitor.

Politics

The Fifth Republic, which has lasted since 1958, was essentially the creation of Charles de Gaulle.

The head of state, who is the President, is elected by universal suffrage for a term of seven years. He selects the Prime Minister and other ministers. He is Chairman of the Cabinet, and Commander of the Armed Forces.

The head of government is the Prime Minister, who is also the leader of the parliament. This is divided into two houses: the National Assembly and the Senate. The National Assembly, which has the power to reverse Senate decisions, is elected by an unusual two-round majority system every five years. The Senate is elected for nine years by an electoral college.

The system is complex, unwieldy and unique. It is matched only by a bureaucracy which de Gaulle suggested was 'almost unworkably complex and massively overstaffed'. The French generally accept that since those heady post-war days the situation has continued to deteriorate. The national joke is that there is no need to fill in a form when five will do the job perfectly well.

Only the French could create such a hierarchy and make it work with any measure of success. That it does has much to do with the ability of successive presidents to cut through red tape. The master of the modern era was Gisgard d'Estaing (1974–81) whose ability to disregard bureaucratic and diplomatic protocols made him massively popular.

The law
Founded on the principles of the Code Napoleon for administrative justice, there are now 'codes' – circulars, decrees and statutes – covering all aspects of French law.

Essentially there are two systems – the administrative and the judiciary. Administrative justice is about settling disputes between individuals and the government. The judiciary deals with civil and criminal cases.

There are levels of tribunals and courts which give French citizens high levels of legal protection. There is no jury system but a mixed tribunal of (three) professional and (six) lay judges. Four of the judges must agree to secure a conviction.

Crime

In common with most EU countries crime in France has increased markedly in recent years. The crime rate, however, particularly in respect of violent crime, is lower than the UK's. But in one area the French top the Euro league for criminal activity. Indeed the theft of vehicles and their contents is now so endemic that incidents are rarely investigated. New sports cars and executive models are often loaded aboard ferries from the south of France to Africa before their theft is reported. Alarms and immobilisers do little to deter professional thieves. Most recently there has been concern about the number of gas attacks (usually ether) at aires and picnic sites. Foreign registered cars and motorcaravans are popular targets.

Highway 'pirates' also target foreign drivers. This crime, which is invariably committed at night, involves gangs who set up road blocks, deliberately cause an accident, or simply ram a vehicle off the road. In each scenario the intention is to make the driver stop. Pirates will then pose as policemen or customs officers. In the worst cases the victims are left naked at the roadside, while the pirates escape with their vehicle and its contents.

Certain young *émigrés* target their own nationals. This may typically be an individual or gang who identify UK licence plates in car parks or slow moving traffic and approach the vehicle and its occupants. They will then play on 'national solidarity and sympathy' (perhaps complaining that they have themselves been victims of crime) to gain access to cash or valuables. The French police are not particularly sympathetic to UK citizens who have been robbed by their compatriots.

Tougher sentencing – the French prison population has doubled to 60,000 in the past decade – has not made a noticeable difference. Housebreaking and burglary have increased, particularly in areas which feature an above average number of second or holiday homes. Mugging has become endemic in some southern towns. Pick pocketing is a plague in Paris. Bag snatching is the curse of Marseille. Truffle rustling has become a problem in the Périgord.

The Côte d'Azur is the crime capital of Europe. Here, a criminal underworld (Milieu) controls robbery, drug trafficking, money laundering, gambling and prostitution. Gang murders and mutilations are commonplace in Marseille where separatist groups – such as the *Front Libéral National Corse* (the Corsican National Liberation Front) – also operate. In contrast to this there are areas of France – as culturally diverse as Alsace and Aquitaine – where violent crime is almost unheard of. You pay your money – or your insurance premiums – and take your choice.

The economy
Although France was subjected to the bite of world

economic recession in the early 1990s, price and wage controls helped to minimise unemployment and sustain a large sector of public employees. At the turn of the millennium France still maintained the largest number of central and local government workers in Europe.

The French economy is based on the bedrock of the fifth most successful industrial country in the world. Agriculture is diverse. Tourism generates vast amounts of foreign exchange. France's future as a major economic power should remain secure if the country can remain a leader in industries such as aerospace and electronics. It is also sobering to note that whereas the UK has pretty much given up on volume vehicle manufacturing (except as a provider of economic labour for the Americans, Germans and Japanese) France remains the base for three of the most innovative and successful car marques in the world (Citroen, Renault and Peugeot).

TO BUY OR NOT TO BUY?

Buy in haste, repent at leisure

Buying property is the biggest single financial commitment that most people make. If that property is in another country, it is wise to be doubly sure that this obligation is understood. Awareness of possible snags and pitfalls is an important part of the process of planning the purchase. For many people it can mean the difference between pleasure of ownership and disaster. The simple fact is that half of all UK buyers of French property will sell up and return to Britain within three years.

There are no surveys definitive enough to determine why this is, but there is strong anecdotal evidence to suggest that these factors include:

◆ Finding the language barrier too great.

◆ Discovering that they, or their children, have simply not settled to living year-round in a foreign country.

◆ Finding that – in rural areas in particular – life is just a touch too '*tranquille*'.

◆ Finding that the winter climate, particularly close to the north and west coasts, and in areas affected by the Massif Central, is more severe than expected.

◆ Finding that decisions made about the purchase of a particular property, particularly in terms of location, were ill-informed and incomplete.

Consider renting first

It is highly recommended that prospective French house buyers rent property first. Short-term letting, especially during peak holiday periods, can be pricey. Longer term arrangements – over a period of six months or more – are well worth considering.

Renting has other advantages:

◆ You are not tying up capital or borrowing large sums of money.

◆ You have a chance to research fully the local property market.

◆ You have time to find out how well you and your family adapt to a new way of life.

◆ You can see if life in the winter lives up to the expectations of the summer.

A giant step

Are you ready to make the leap across the Channel? It may be only 22 miles of water, but for the unprepared it can be a huge psychological and cultural barrier. There are no English subtitles on French TV.

Prospective purchasers of French property typically fall into one of four groups:

◆ Someone 'seconded' by his company, or an entrepreneur developing his interests in the wider European market.

◆ Those looking for a second or holiday home.

◆ Those wishing to retire abroad or moving to a 'better' climate for health reasons.

◆ Escapers, dreamers, good-lifers, and various styles and shades of creative talent.

These categories invariably overlap. Perhaps someone approaching retirement who buys a second home with a view to making it a first if he can sell some paintings, is as reliable a stereotype as any.

Whatever category you place yourself in the advice remains the same: do not buy a property in France until you fully understand what you are letting yourself in for.

A second home

If you are considering a second home, but have never owned one before, ask yourself the following questions:

◆ Will you get enough use from the property? A second home is an all year-round expense.

◆ Will you want to spend all your holidays in the same place?

◆ Will the travelling put you off taking short breaks there?

◆ What size property do you want? Do you really need five extra bedrooms for all those friends who have said they may visit?

◆ How much of your holiday time are you prepared to devote to repairs, decorating and cleaning out gutters?

◆ Will you let others use the property in your absence? And, if they pay, how might this affect your mortgage/tax position?

◆ Do you need a caretaker, gardener or cleaner? Who will oversee repairs and renovations in your absence?

◆ What arrangements need to be made for the property when not in use? Britain does not have a monopoly on crime and empty property is attractive to criminals. Some household insurance policies are invalid if a property is unoccupied for more than 30 consecutive days.

Relocating to France

If you are considering moving lock, stock and barrel, ask yourself these further questions before you commit to anything:

◆ What is your chosen region like in both January and July? A chalet in the Jura is idyllic in the late spring, but perhaps less so after two weeks of January blizzards.

◆ Do you have the full support of your family? Will your wealthy aunt cut you off without a penny now she can no longer invite you to Sunday lunch?

◆ Have you thought through the implications for taxation, healthcare and education?

◆ Will you be able to find work and/or transfer sufficient funds to live on?

◆ Is your French adequate for day-to-day communication?

NEED TO KNOW

Before you begin house hunting there are a number of things you need to know. These include:

◆ personal taxation

◆ registration tax

◆ capital gains tax

◆ nationality and naturalisation

◆ rights as a European citizen

- working in France

- estate agents and notaries

- building in France

- banking and finance

- disputes and litigation

- maintaining the vernacular

- the legal process of purchase

- surveys and planning permission

- renting and running your property

- legal responsibilities.

Later sections of this book deal with each of these.

Do not be put off by what seems to be an encyclopedia of knowledge. The French do things differently, but the approach is generally based on common sense and the legal process is designed to protect you.

Price

A potential French buyer reads an advertised price, particularly on older property, as a starting point for driving a hard bargain. They know that the asking price is optimistic. They also know that, although prices are higher in the south, this creates increased room for manoeuvre. There is absolutely no rule which prevents a potential UK buyer from taking a similarly robust approach.

Here are some further general pointers:

◆ Although the asking price is invariable more than the final selling price it may be difficult to judge how much room there is to negotiate. Be prepared to walk away from a deal while showing enthusiasm for the property itself. Leave a telephone number and wait for a call. The outcome may be surprising.

◆ French estate agents (agents immobilier) are well aware of the buying whims of their UK customers. In some areas you will find agents with window displays in English. This is not because of the *entente cordiale*.

◆ New properties are more expensive than older ones.

◆ Brand new apartments and condominiums are expensive. They are invariably built on prime sites in fashionable areas.

◆ Older apartments and condominiums are variably priced. Much depends on the age and condition of the whole building. This is a sector of the market which requires caution. It is this kind of property that was most affected by the recession of the early 1990s.

◆ Property values decrease according to remoteness. In the same region you may find a large country house in the same price range as a seaside apartment.

◆ Regions, particular towns and villages, and even certain streets are 'fashionable'. This is always reflected in the price.

◆ As French estate agents charge the seller or the buyer around 5% for their services; it is often possible to save this amount (or more) by buying direct. Local newspapers are often a good place to start for prospective buyers. Up to 40% of French properties are 'sold' through small ads and word of mouth.

◆ A small garden – un petit jardin – has a different meaning on each side of the Channel. We tend to think of something a bit bigger than a window box, the French regard it as something that does not require the services of a full-time gardener.

◆ Registration fees are lower on properties that are less than five years old. The full legal process of purchase, including surveys and planning applications, is likely to add 10 to 15% to the agreed sale price.

WHAT CHOICE IS THERE?

There is property in Franch to suit all pockets and lifestyles. The single most common type of property in all areas is the '*pavilion*'. This is a detached family house set in a fairly large (by English standards) garden and usually with a *sous-sol* (underground area) that acts as a laundry room, garage, cellar and junk-room.

French estate agents maintain databases of properties that are more up to date than the free magazine style property guides racked up outside the offices. Always ask for a list rather than a guide and ask to be added to the mailing list. Some agents place sample advertisements in English newspapers and on English language websites. In some cases this is little more than a ruse to add a potential UK buyer to their mailing list.

Making the right choice

But the estate agent's window is the prime source of information once you have made the decision to buy. Studied carefully, it can tell you almost all you need to know about the local property market.

Even if you don't speak French it is possible to work out general facts about a property. French properties are advertised typically as T1, T3 or T6. This is short for Type 1, Type 3 or Type 6. The digit refers to the number of principal rooms. A T4 therefore could be a three-bedroomed dwelling with a living room or a two-bedroomed one with a separate lounge and dining room.

Within a fairly narrow price band a range of lifestyles is amply demonstrated by the five properties featured below. Each has its own attractions so it is important that the buyer is sure exactly what he is looking for. Nothing is more likely to bring a look of despair to a French estate agent's face than you offering no guideline beyond price. In England the motto may well be 'you pay your money and take your choice'; for the French it is the other way round!

All these properties can be found in and around a pleasant market town on the banks of the Loire and were listed in the same agency in October 2002. They were featured as 'free of agent's charges' (i.e. the vendor pays the agency fee).

The first is a stone-built property situated 300 metres from the town centre:

A traditional house of 130m^2, 4 bedrooms, fully equipped kitchen, bathroom, 2 WCs. Of very good quality construction with an open fireplace in the lounge and a separate living room. The property has full double glazing, two garages, a cellar and an attic. French windows in the living room give onto 30m^2 of covered terrace and a further 60m^2 of uncovered terrace. The central heating is electric. The property stands in 1620m^2 of land. The garden is walled with mature trees. Asking price €162,000.

Figure 2. French estate agent's descrition (1).

The second is in a small village about 10 miles from the same town:

A four bedroom split-level property covering 150m^2. The property features a fully equipped kitchen, two bathrooms and two separate WCs. There is a lounge with a log burning fireplace and separate living room which gives onto a south-facing terrace. Heating is by gas. The property, which is constructed on 2000m^2 of land is situated close to local shops in an historic village. Asking price €128,000.

Figure 3. French estate agent's property description (2).

The third is a modern property constructed close to the town's outer ring-road:

Building of recent construction of 90m². There are three bedrooms, a bathroom, separate WC, a family room, heat and sound insulation, a water softener, electric central heating, a small terrace, and a designated parking place covered by CCTV cameras. Asking price €115,000.

Figure 4. French estate agent's property description (3).

Next is a substantial rural property some 12 miles from the town, with the nearest village two miles distant:

Partly renovated farm buildings set in 0.8 hectare with a barn suitable for conversion. The main building consists of five bedrooms, two living rooms, a traditional style kitchen with log-burning stove and back boiler, a vestibule and hallway, one bathroom with WC, separate WC, pantry and cellar. Lean-to garage and log store adjoin main building. Barn approx 110m² floor space. Small orchard and fishing pond. Gravelled track to main road. Asking price €142,000.

Figure 5. French estate agent's property description (4).

And finally, here is an apartment close to the town centre:

Recently constructed T3 apartment on third floor of five storey building. Master bedroom with en-suite facilities, separate bathroom and WC. Fitted kitchen with waste disposal. Recessed lighting in living area. Electric central heating. Balcony overlooks historic town square. Underground secure garaging for one vehicle. Additional secure parking by negotiation at extra cost. Asking price €141,000.

Figure 6. French estate agent's property description (5).

Where and what to buy

Before diving into the French property market there are a number of matters to consider.

THE REGIONS

Some buyers may have already homed in on a geographical target area, others may prefer to begin by investigating the relative merits of different regions.

According to one chain of national estate agents the most popular regions with the British are:

◆ The Pas de Calais and the coastal strip of Picardy around Boulogne and Le Touquet.

◆ Normandy, particularly around Deauville and Honfleur.

◆ Brittany, especially the coastal strips between St Malo and Roscoff, Quimper and Vannes.

◆ The Loire valley in general, but mainly around Tours and Blois.

◆ Charente and Charente Maritime.

◆ The Dordogne.

◆ Gascony.

◆ Provence in general, but especially the Vaucluse and the areas around Nimes and Aix-en-Provence.

◆ Burgundy.

◆ The Vosges.

◆ Languedoc.

Target areas

Many buyers of French property have a good idea of their target area. Sometimes they have friends in a certain area, or they have already rented a *gîte*.

It is surprising however that many people do not investigate the merits of different parts of the country. Each region has its own character and will score differently in a personal checklist of advantages and disadvantages.

TARGET POINTERS

It is perhaps appropriate at this point for you to ask yourself what your priorities are. If you have not decided upon a region, your priorities and the thumbnail sketches that follow may well help. First try listing the phrases below in your own order of preference:

◆ easy access by car

◆ climate is warm and sunny all year round

◆ area is quiet and suitable for most country pursuits

◆ plenty of cultural/historical opportunities nearby

◆ close to the sea

◆ close to rail/air links

◆ area suitable for children

◆ area good for specialist hobbies e.g. golf, fishing.

Each of the most popular areas has its aficionados; much depends upon your personal choice.

	Calais	Cherbourg	Le Havre	St Malo	Roscoff
Amiens	55	180	110	235	330
Caen	220	85	70	115	210
Rennes	290	150	135	50	280
Tours	325	215	190	180	275
Saintes	465	345	330	180	450
Souillac	500	430	420	370	440
Mont de Marsan	625	480	490	400	470
Avignon	650	570	570	590	680
Dijon	490	500	410	470	460
Colmar	400	540	430	540	640

Figure 7. Mileage chart – regional centres and main ports.

The mileage chart (Figure 7) may help you decide which area to begin with. The mileages are approximate. The towns/cities listed in the left hand column could be considered as central to the ten main regions.

Figure 8.   Regional hotspots.

The prices under each entry in Fig. 9 are for a typical T3 apartment, the first entry being purchase price and the second a monthly rental figure.

The inconsistency of these values reflects the difficulty in assessing the market. The prices below were quoted by accredited agents but only the barest details of the condition and precise location of each property were given. In each case the rental indicated was for long-term lets (six months or more) but higher returns could be achieved, particularly during the holiday season.

The Pas de Calais and the coastal strip of Picardie around Boulogne and Le Touquet	*Boulogne* €120,000	€1,200
Normandy, particularly around Deauville and Honfleur	*Cabourg* €85,000	€800
Brittany, especially the coastal strips between St Malo and Roscoff, Quimper and Vannes	*Lannion* €162,000	€550
The Loire Valley in general, but mainly around Tours and Blois	*Tours* €82,000	€500
Charente and Charente Maritime	*Royan* €110,000	€650
Paris	*Montmatre* €290,000	€1500
The Dordogne and Lot	*Cahors* €165,000	€595
Gironde	*Bordeaux* €190,000	€725
Provence in general but especially Vaucluse and the areas around Nimes and Aix-en-Provence	*Aix-en-Provence* €190,000	€850
Burgundy	*Dijon* €95,000	€650
Vosges	*Epinal* €95,000	€550
Languedoc	*Montpellier* €180,000	€990

Figure 9. Regional hotspots – prices for a typical T3 apartment.

Invariably rural areas provide the greatest bargains. These are generally the parts of France where agriculture once bloomed and the population rose rapidly during the last two centuries.

More recent and ever increasing industrialisation had pushed this population trend into reverse and created an over supply of country properties. Best value buys were in the Limousin, the Ardeche, Haute Vienne, Cantal, Les Landes and Nevers.

In recent years the French themselves have begun to discover:

◆ Aquitaine: the 'new Loire'. For those who find the draw of chateaux and their gardens irresistible.

◆ The Auvergne: the upper reaches in particular around les Mondeux have become popular with those who prefer a slightly more '*tranquille*' ski experience.

◆ France-Comte: an increasingly popular summer location that features two superb forests (Foret de la Joux, Foret de la Fresse), a classic view point (Pic de l'aigle) and the much photographed Lac de Chalain.

◆ Poitou-Charentes: this area, after the Côte d'Azur, has the greatest concentration of French holiday homes. The old town of La Rochelle attracts large visitor numbers, particularly in the summer. Saintes is charming, elegant and steeped in history, La Palmyre is the best zoo in Europe and the beaches around Royan are perhaps the finest in France.

Consider which region of France best fits your profile and budget. The following thumbnail descriptions may help.

The Pas de Calais and Picardy

Most visitors see only the less attractive areas around the ports of Calais and Dunkirk from the autoroute. Of all the French regions though, this has the greatest concentration of British-owned property. The advantageous price differential was somewhat eroded when the British property market declined alongside the value of the pound in the late 1980s.

Although not obviously attractive to visitors there are some 'undiscovered' gems, such as Montreuil-sur-Mer and the delightful Poix de Picardie.

Advantages Transport links, easy access, reasonable prices
The downside Weather, plain countryside, 'booze cruise Brits'

Normandy

There is good access to the UK through Caen, Cherbourg and Le Havre. In the late 1990s bargains were picked up by the British, particularly around Honfleur and Deauville. Consequently local builders earned a good living renovating inexpensive cottages. The situation has changed recently but there are still bargains to be had particularly in larger rural properties.

Coastal property is relatively expensive particularly around Ouistreham, Trouville and Deauville. There is better value to be had on the Cotentin peninsular. Inland and to the south there are still some bargains in the area known as Petit

Suisse (particularly around Clecy) in the Orne valley. Prices generally increase in areas most accessible from Paris for a weekend retreat.

Advantages Rolling countryside, half-timbered houses, access

The downside Few coastal bargains, English weather, British enclaves

Britanny
Brittany is more difficult to access but it remains justifiably popular with British buyers. The influence of the Gulf Stream makes part of the coast, especially in the north and west, remarkably mild for the latitude.

The area around St Malo, Dinard and Dinan is delightful but prices reflect this. There are better bargains to be had along the coast westwards towards Roscoff where there are some sheltered gems of seaside villages such as St Jacut de la Mer. It should be remembered that the western Brittany peninsular (Finisterre) suffers the worst of the winter Atlantic gales and that towns such as Brest and Quimper are almost as distant from the Channel ports as the south of France. The southern parts of Brittany and Loire Atlantic are more accessible and have a milder winter climate. The coastal strip from La Baule through St Nazaire and across the Loire estuary to Pornic is popular with the French themselves for second homes. Letting values here are considered to be a good return on property investment although holiday letting is limited to a relatively short season.

Advantages Dramatic coastline, seafood, Breton culture
The downside Atlantic gales, impossible to remember place
names

The Loire Valley

The Loire river is said to be a major climatic division. It is certainly true to say that during the summer months the influence of the midi (the south) is noticeable.

The Loire valley is also known as the market garden of France. It is an area rich in history and is very much on the tourist itinerary. Routes to the Loire from Channel ports are not good but the new motorway link from Alençon to Rouen will improve matters. Some popular centres such as Saumur and Amboise have become hugely popular with the British. The French themselves have a high regard for Tours. There are also some delightful small towns such as Loches, Montrichard, Chinon, La Fleche and Ingrandes.

Advantages Steeped in history, iridescent light, classy towns
The downside On the US tourist trail, winter woollies
required

Champagne-Ardennes

The area has two distinctive characters – the upland forests of the Ardennes and the undulating chalk fields of Champagne. There are some lovely villages and pleasant walled towns, such as Langres and Leon. Property prices are competitive and the area is almost undiscovered by the British.

The advantages Access to northern Europe, some bargain
   properties
The downside Cold winters, moist summers

Charente and Charente Maritime

This area has opened up recently because of improved
motorway links. Unfortunately this means it has become
increasingly popular with British buyers. In the more rural
areas, however, there is still a plentiful supply of relatively
inexpensive property and the area is worth considering for
those with a limited budget.

The area around Cognac and Saintes attracts the majority
of inland buyers while properties in the (more expensive)
fishing ports and holiday towns, and islands to the north-
west are frequently the choice of seasonal visitors. The area
bordering on the Limousin, immediately north-west of
Angouleme (around Ruffec) represents excellent value
although the (short) winters can be bitterly cold. Indeed
temperatures have fallen to $-16°C$ in recent years.

Advantages Inexpensive property, best sunbathing coast in
   France
The downside Wet and windy winter, becoming popular with
   the British

Midi-Pyrennees

A massive area comprising the French sector of the
Pyrennees, the south-western corner of the Massif Central
and the long valley in between. Toulouse, astride the Canal
du Midi and Garonne, is the natural capital of the region.

The Pyrennees, still regarded by some as Europe's final wild frontier, has been massively developed for snow sports and climbing. There are few property bargains here. Toulouse itself is fairly pricey and properties on the coastal strip around Perpignan and Argeles sur Mer are around twice the price of those encountered on the nearby (Spanish) Costa Brava.

Advantages Good year-round coastal climate, excellent letting potential

The downside Fairly pricey property, long distance by road

The Limousin and Auvergne

Known as '*La France Profonde*' (deep France), the Auvergne has also been described as France's 'Wild West'. The volcanic landscape is breathtaking, with villages such as Orcival rivalling any in the country for character. Winter woollies are required but it may be worth it for the best value (and cheapest) property in France. The improved motorway links have made the Auvergne a recent target for bargain hunters, but this is a thinly populated area so the buyer may find himself exploring far from the beaten track.

The Limousin has lakes, gorges and forests. For *la vie tranquille* it scores at the top of the scale and its colourful capital, Limoges, is steeped in history. As with the Auvergne, prices are low but beginning to climb as the British discover it.

Advantages Rural beauty and solitude, best bargains in property

The downside Access, short sharp winters, British enclaves

The Dordogne and Lot Valleys

The Dordogne is one of France's longest and most beautiful rivers. The most attractive area between Bort-les-Orgues and Beaulieu-sur-Dordogne is also the most expensive. Better value can be had closer to the Lot. The Dordogne was one of the first areas in France to attract significant numbers of UK buyers. The area is now home to second and third generation British nationals with a predominance of ex-academics and ex-military, often recognisable by their vintage Panama hats and similarly battered Volvos. The Dordogne Ladies Club and the Dordogne Organisation of Gentlemen (DOGS) each have their own committees with rules carefully framed to avoid using the word 'class'. This should be taken as a clear signal to the 'wrong sort of people' that they simply do not belong here. The summer cricket festival at Eynet is a highlight of the social calendar.

The Dordogne is also the cauldron of France. Its high summer temperatures and humidity are either attractive or unbearable, depending on your preferences. The upper reaches of the region (towards the Auvergne) offer a more temperate summer climate.

The Lot Valley, particularly around Cahors, is well worth considering. Values are certain to increase when the west-east motorway link from Périgueux to Clermont-Ferrand is complete.

Advantages Pleasant climate all year round, best markets in France

The downside Fairly pricey, try parking in August

Gascony

This ancient duchy, later part of Aquitaine and hence formerly the birthright of British kings, has recently become fashionable for Britains wishing to set up home in France. Following a steep rise in property prices in the Dordogne and Languedoc, Gascony is fast becoming the latest enclave of ex-patriot British people.

The coast, from Bordeaux to Biarritz, is virtually one flat sandy beach which offers the best surfing in Europe. Indeed, that same beach begins geographically as far north as Soulac (near Royan) and runs almost without interruption to the Spanish border at Hendaye Plage.

In contrast, inland, there are miles and miles of forest all virtually empty. The northern part of the territory is wine country, including such famous names as the Chateaux Latour, Chateaux Lafitte and Chateaux d'Yquem. To the south are the foothills of the Pyrenees and the Basque country.

The climate is generally mild and frost free in winter. Even the summer heat is tempered by Atlantic breezes. That part of the coast known as Les Landes seems uninhabited other than by mosquitoes with vampire instincts. Properties between Biarritz and the Spanish border are much sought after and consequently expensive. The best bargains are to be had along the corridor of the N134 between Roquefort and Pau.

Advantages Biarritz in June, red wines, Spanish neighbours
The downside Mosquitoes, Biarritz in August, Spanish neighbours

Inland Provence

Good motorway links have made the area accessible. The climate is good all year round apart from the few weeks when the Mistral blows down the Rhone valley. Even before Peter Mayle, Provence was a popular choice with British buyers. Property prices reflect this, particularly in the Vaucluse and around Nîmes and Aix-en-Provence.

Although this is not an area for the bargain hunter, it could still be regarded as value for money for buyers considering letting. Best value (again according to FNAIM figures) can be found around Ales, Vaison-la-Romaine, Bollene and Pont-St-Esprit.

Advantages Lavender breezes, steeped in history, climate
The downside The mistral, prices, UK enclaves, Peter Mayle

The Côte d'Azur

The Côte d'Azur has been the summer playground for wealthy Britains for more than a century. Villas on the Cap d'Antibes appear to be reserved for minor royalty, geriatric pop stars and lottery winners. A modest apartment at Cagnes sur Mer is rather more affordable. As you go westwards the towns become less fashionable and property is consequently cheaper.

Advantages Hot dry summers, excellent beaches, air access
The downside Warm wet winters, known as 'the coast of crime'

Burgundy

Burgundy offers fine wines and gourmet cuisine. It is a land of rich pastures and golden villages, which makes it both picturesque and pricey. Burgundy also has a network of navigable waterways little used commercially but ideal for messing about in boats. Thanks to the limited inroads that tourism has made into the region there may still be some property bargains, particularly in the upland area, the Jura, which is known as 'old France'. Prices increase with proximity to the Swiss border.

Advantages Almost unspoilt, picture postcard scenery
The downside Becoming pricey, long winters

The Vosges

The Vosges region again reflects the huge variety of what France can offer the property buyer. Although interest in this hilly and wooded region has increased in recent years there are still bargains to be had. Delightful villages such as Bussang, Ferrette, La Hohwald, St Amerin and Schirmeck vie for the attention of the buyer with the popular larger resort towns of Masevaux and Plombieres les Bains.

The Vosges is particularly popular with nature lovers and walkers who enjoy peace and unspoilt countryside. The names of towns and villages in the region indicate the historic links with Germany and this is reflected in the local wine and food. The Vosges is also becoming increasingly popular as a winter location although the road infrastructure is by no means as good as the Alps. Property prices are slightly above average.

Advantages Some bargain properties, Germanic style and tradition

The downside The roads in winter, summer midges, poor
access

The Rhone Alps

The area, which lies between Lyon and the Swiss border is
popular for both winter and summer sports. The summer
weather is less certain than in the far south but is generally
good. The snow-capped mountains tell you all you need to
know about the winters. Holiday letting potential is excellent
but property bargains are scarce.

Advantages Excellent letting potential, year round postcard
views
The downside Winter access problems, expensive property

Languedoc

The Languedoc has arguably the best climate in France,
which may begin to explain why, for the British, the
Languedoc is the new Dordogne. This hotspot status has
encouraged prices to rise rapidly with agents claiming a near
30% increase in the years 2001 to 2002.

Carcassonne (known as 'Corkassonnay' by some of the
British contingent) has become so popular that, despite
the proximity of airports at Toulouse and Perpignan, it is
now also accessed by scheduled flights. Prices in the more
popular corners of Languedoc are as high as anywhere in
France outside Paris.

The Languedoc has also attracted buyers who have been
'pushed' along the Côte d'Azur by property prices. You will
pay a premium in seaside towns like Narbonne-Plage but

there are still relative bargains to be had in and around Montpellier.

Advantages Climate and culture, access by air, Montpellier
The downside Some pricey property, the British contingent

Paris

Buyers should generally avoid the suburbs and take care when purchasing in the popular ninth *arrondissement*. Only the most desirable apartments on the Mediterranean coast and luxury chalet-style apartments in the Alps produce better letting returns and in both these cases the initial investment is likely to be considerably greater. A 50 square metre apartment would cost typically around €170,000 and could quite realistically return €1,700 net per month gross letting income.

The ninth Arrondisement, which includes Montmartre and the Pigalle, needs to be interpreted on a street by street basis in order to determine whether the area is 'chic' or 'colourful'. As both driving and parking in Paris are the stuff of nightmares, close access to the metro and bus routes are very important.

Advantages Paris in the Spring, high letting values, a touch of culture
The downside Paris in the Winter, parking at any time, queues for everything

The following temperature summary chart may also prove useful. Average daily maximum and minimum temperatures are indicated in centigrade.

	Spring	Summer	Autumn	Winter
Bordeaux	17/6	25/14	18/8	9/2
Boulogne	12/6	20/14	18/8	6/0
Lyon	16/6	27/15	16/7	5/-2
Nantes	16/6	24/14	16/8	8/2
Nice	17/9	27/18	21/12	13/4
Paris	16/6	26/15	16/7	6/1
Strasbourg	16/5	25/13	14/6	2/-2

Figure 10.   Temperature summary chart.

Here the annual rainfall is given in millimetres and sunshine as average daily hours.

	Rainfall	Sunshine
Biarritz	1475	6.3
Nantes	668	5.3
Nice	579	7.5
Paris	619	5.0

Figure 11.   Rain or shine.

THE FRENCH MOTORWAY NETWORK
Although the network is perhaps not quite up to the standard of Germany and Belgium, most UK drivers will find the French motorways a delight when compared with the crumbling infrastructure in the UK.

The most recent motorways are toll roads and will generally remain so until the construction costs have been paid. A feature of French motorways are regular 'aires' for resting, leg-stretching, picnicking, showering, etc. Some aires have commercial services such as those found at motorway service stations in the UK.

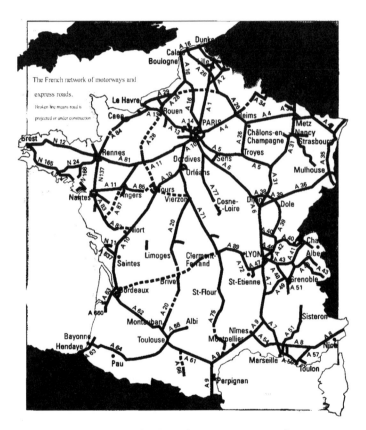

Figure 12. The French motorway network.

FLYING TO YOUR DESTINATION

France has more international standard airports than any other European country. However, London apart, access from Britain's regions is patchy and some low-cost operators use airports that are miles distant from the cities they purport to serve.

Many provincial British airports have flights direct to their French regional counterparts. Although air transport to France has been historically expensive the situation has changed because of the low-cost alternatives. If Geneva, for these purposes, is included as a 'French regional airport' there are now 24 low-cost destinations. What follows is a 'snapshot' of these. Both fares quoted are return. The best price advertised will usually only apply to mid-week flights booked well in advance. The fare quoted for weekends is for 'leave on Friday and return on Sunday' bookings.

Destination	Departure	'Best price (€)	Weekend (€)
Bégerac	Stanstead	95	262
Biarritz	Stanstead	83	158
Bordeaux	Stanstead	95	193
Brest	Stanstead	88	131
Caen	Stanstead	69	124
Carcassonne	Stanstead	131	192
Chambéry	Stanstead	193	267
Dinard	Stanstead	81	155
Geneva	Birmingham	60	60
	Cardiff		
	East Midlands		

	Gatwick		
	Liverpool		
	Luton		
	Stanstead		
Grenoble	Stanstead	93	144
La Rochelle	Stanstead	70	90
Limoges	Stanstead	93	144
Lyon	Stanstead	99	99
St Etienne	Stanstead	78	131
Marseille	Stanstead	92	199
Montpellier	Stanstead	67	199
Nice	Bristol	77	210
	East Midlands		
	Gatwick		
	Liverpool		
	Luton		
	Stanstead		
Nimes	Stanstead	66	141
Perpignan	Stanstead	99	265
Poitiers	Stanstead	71	69
Strasbourg	Stanstead	155	160
Toulon	Stanstead	94	199
Toulouse	East Midlands	81	190
	Stanstead		
	Newcastle		
Tours	Stanstead	71	85

Figure 13. The cost of flying to French regional airports.

Figure 14. French destinations served by low-cost airlines

THE RAILWAYS

The French national railway system – the SNCF – offers frequent and efficient train services even to small towns and villages. The new inter-city fast train network – the TGV – is one of the most remarkable and successful engineering projects of modern times. It cost billions and the French are outrageously proud of it.

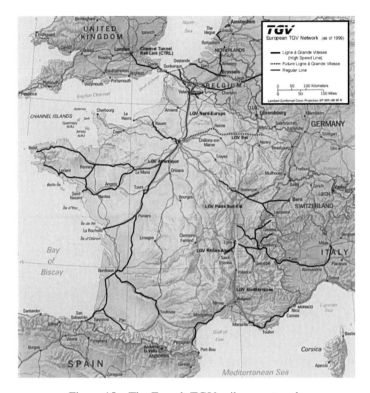

Figure 15.   The French TGV railway network.

For those familiar with the cost and vagaries of railway travel in the UK the French railway experience is a delight even in anticipation.

PRICE GUIDELINES

It is impossible to be precise about how much you would expect to pay for a French property. This is because variations within regions themselves can be considerable.

In general terms your money will buy:

◆ Up to €35,000 a barn or small farmhouse requiring renovation.

◆ Up to €50,000 a studio apartment in a popular resort.
A partly restored cottage in a rural area.

◆ Up to €80,000 a substantial farmhouse requiring renovation.
A one bedroom apartment in a popular town.
A partly restored three bedroom rural property.

◆ Up to €100,000 a restored three bedroom rural property.
A modern two bedroom property.
A three bedroomed restored farmhouse.
A tasteful rural barn conversion.
A one bedroom apartment in a popular resort.

◆ Up to €150,000 a fully restored four bedroom farmhouse.
A fully restored rural property with a swimming pool.
A two bedroomed apartment in a popular resort.
A tasteful barn conversion with an orchard and pool.

◆ Up to €200,000 a three bedroomed apartment in a popular resort.
A fully restored four bedroom farmhouse and pool.
A studio apartment in a fashionable part of Paris.
A two bedroomed apartment in the Alps.
A small chateau in need of some renovation.

◆ Up to €350,000 a two bedroomed apartment on the Champs Elysee.
A luxury apartment at a popular resort.

A modest but partly restored chateau.

A most respectable villa with a pool in Provence.

A luxury three bedroom chalet in the Alps.

The following tables may provide more valuable guidelines. They summarise comprehensive returns from ten major towns and their surrounding districts. However, although these figures were compiled in 2004 they should be treated with caution. They nevertheless make a useful comparison for various property types. They are rounded to the nearest square metre.

It may be helpful to know that a three to four bedroom house with a garage is likely to be around 180 square metres, a typical three bedroom bungalow around 120 square metres, and a holiday style two bedroom bungalow around 80 square metres.

Using the tables below you could calculate, for example, that the cost of an average sized (120 square metre) renovated house in the town centre of Bordeaux would be: 1,610 x 120 = €194,400.

Or that a renovated house of similar size in the Bordeaux city suburbs would be: 1105 x 120 = €132,600.

Town centre

	Unrestored	Renovated	New
Bordeaux	1000	1620	2175
Clermont-Ferrand	1000	1250	1690
Dijon	1125	1290	1745
Lille	780	1170	1630
Lyon	1115	1400	2025
Marseille	630	1120	1725
Nantes	840	1330	1825
Orleans	950	1190	1695
Rouen	930	1450	1985
Strasbourg	1260	1550	2230
Average	**965**	**1360**	**1870**

Figure 16. Property prices (town centre).

Suburban

	Unrestored	Renovated	New
Bordeaux	920	1105	1440
Clermont-Ferrand	770	955	1220
Dijon	800	930	1275
Lille	665	860	1070
Lyon	850	1100	1430
Marseille	650	915	1165
Nantes	805	1050	1295
Orleans	840	1095	1210
Rouen	900	1135	1390
Strasbourg	970	1210	1585
Average	**820**	**1035**	**1180**

Figure 17. Property prices (suburban).

Rural district

	Unrestored	Renovated	New
Bordeaux	495	785	1175
Clermont-Ferrand	415	580	860
Dijon	470	580	970
Lille	330	575	800
Lyon	500	680	1120
Marseille	350	570	980
Nantes	430	590	970
Orleans	380	520	710
Rouen	555	665	1060
Strasbourg	550	695	1100
Average	**450**	**625**	**875**

Figure 18.   Property prices (rural).

(*The surveys were carried out by Macdonald Research recently. At least three agencies in each town were asked to provide data.*)

Conclusions

Althought there are inconsistencies, it is possible to draw the following general conclusions:

◆ Suburban properties are around 75% of town centre values.

◆ Rural properties are around 50% of town centre values.

◆ The cost of a new property is often almost twice the price of an unrestored one.

Stability

Beware of the kind of 'boom and bust' journalism which responds to fairly localised property value increases as an indicator of the wider market. This only adds to a false perception of the bigger picture. Overall, the French property market remains more stable and predictable than our own. This stability is predicted to continue, though fashion has dictated some rapidly changing values in some areas.

BUYING AT AUCTION

UK buyers are generally suspicious of buying at auction (*ventes aux echères*) but this remains a likely way of securing a bargain. Properties for auction are most frequently found in rural areas and are likely to require restoration. There is unlikely to be a great deal of competition at the sale.

Most of these properties have been the subject of inheritance disputes, intestacy or mortgage lenders' repossessions. The mortgage lenders are primarily interested in recovering their debt as swiftly as possible. The reserve price is invarably around half the estimated market value. Details must be published six weeks before the sale in local newspapers. A standard form (*fiche*) notes the place and date of the sale, the lawyer who is handling it, the reserve price and arrangements for viewing. There is also a brief description of the property and its grounds.

Potential buyers appoint a lawyer registered with the *Tribunal de Grande Instance* to make bids on their behalf. The lawyer seals bids – up to the maximum agreed – in envelopes. A returnable bidding entry fee – usually around

€1,500 – is determined by the auctioneer. At the close of the sale the lawyer must deposit 10% of the purchase price. Other fees – amounting to around 20% of the purchase price – must be paid within a month.

A judge presides at the auction itself. Two lights (equivalent to 'going once, going twice') are lit at each round of bidding. A third light marks the winning bid. In some rural areas the same procedure is still carried out in the more traditional way, with candles replacing the light bulbs. Even more archaic is a ten-day rule which allows further bids to be made. If a higher bid is received, the property must be re-auctioned within 60 days. Happily this intervention, which is very rare, can occur only once.

Although this method of purchase may sound daunting it is well worth considering if the property otherwise fits the bill. Bidding invariably begins at the reserve level and rarely climbs to 70% of the 'estimated market value'.

GARAGING AND PARKING

Modern family houses and most rural properties will have garaging facilities – perhaps in the form of a *sous-sol* – included in the purchase price. However, garaging or private parking is not generally included in either the purchase or rental of an apartment or town house in France.

A lock up garage is likely to cost between €9,000 and €10,500, a permanent reserved parking space between €3,300 and €7,500 or an annual contract for secure covered parking between €1,000 and €1,500.

A parking facility of some kind is essential. Not only is it difficult at certain times to find street parking in cities and popular resorts, but it is worthy recalling that France has the highest incidence in Europe of the theft of both vehicles and their contents.

$$\left(\begin{array}{c}3\end{array}\right)$$

Renting a property and timeshare

Holidays spent in hotels and guest houses can help you decide if an area is suitable for you. But renting a property, especially during the winter months, is both recommended and relatively inexpensive.

HOTELS AND GUEST HOUSES

Hotels in France charge around half as much for a room as you would expect to pay in the UK for two people sharing a room. A hotel – particularly in rural areas – can be easier on the pocket than a *gîte*.

Look out for the sign *Chambre(s) à Louer* hanging in the windows of ordinary domestic property. If the sign is displayed then a room is available, often at a price that would be considered uneconomic in the UK.

It is a French tradition that you are shown accommodation before you decide whether or not to sign the register. This applies to hotels, guest houses, or even a spare bedroom in somebody's home. French law requires that prices of all hotel rooms must be displayed in a prominent place, with minimum and maximum guidelines on the outside of the building.

Lists and details of all available accomodation can be obtained at the local *syndicat d'initiative*.

HOLIDAY LETTING

Gîtes (holiday properties) are advertised in many national UK newspapers, travel agents and via the internet.

They provide furnished self-catering accommodation that can be anything from a chateau to a seaside apartment. They are classified according to the facilities they provide and each local *syndicat d'initiative* (tourist information office) retains a list of properties available in the area. A national federation imposes rules about minimum standards of furnishing and facilities.

The best way to find a *gîte* is frequently through personal recommendation. Be wary of newspaper advertisements. Some of those that appear to offer particular *gîtes* are in fact 'samples' placed by letting agencies. The *gîte* advertised is not usually available, and indeed may not exist. What you will receive, however, is a wad of unsolicited mail frequently offering inferior quality accommodation at grossly inflated prices.

Most reputable companies issue informative brochures. The following can normally be obtained through UK travel agents:

◆ Blakes Villas

◆ Country Holidays in France

◆ The Complete France

◆ Vacances en Campagne

These companies are specialists and offer a wide selection of accommodation at competitive rates. Brittany Ferries also offers a wide range of packages that include *gîte* rental.

Local tourist offices are always willing to send out extensive lists of all forms of accommodation. It is best to restrict your enquiry to the kind of accommodation you need.

Booking direct

This is often the cheapest way to reserve a *gîte*. The problem is that the information you receive from the owner may be sketchy, and in high season the best *gîtes* are frequently reserved from one year to the next.

For your protection it is always best to get a written agreement. Some *gîte* owners send out printed forms.

It is important to be sure about:

♦ The duration of the let and times of arrival and departure.

♦ The deposit. Normally 10% but some owners demand up to 25%.

♦ Arrangements for the payment of services – electricity, water, etc.

♦ The facilities – particularly the numbers of beds and bedrooms.

♦ Exactly what is provided as part of the letting 'package'.

♦ Arrangements for car parking. Many apartments are allocated off-road parking for one vehicle.

♦ Arrangements for picking up and returning keys.

Advance payments

The deposit paid for a *gîte is* either *un acompte* or *arrhes*. The legal distinction is important.

If you cancel after having paid *un acompte* you not only lose the deposit but the *gîte* owner can hold you responsible for the full amount due for the letting period.

If you cancel having paid *arrhes* only the deposit is forfeited.

However, this does not always mean that it is best to have the deposit described as *arrhes*. *Un acompte* means you can make a claim for breach of contract if the *gîte* is unsatisfactory, or if you are denied access. Depending on the circumstances the damages awarded could be considerable. *Arrhes* under French law means that the *gîte* owner will be obliged to pay only twice the deposit you gave him.

The best advice when booking direct is to pay *un acompte* but to ensure that you have holiday insurance that covers you if you are unable to travel.

Tax incentives for gîte owners

There are tax incentives for owners to offer properties as a *gîte*. In order to qualify, the *gîte* has to be available for at least three months of the year. It is not uncommon for the *gîte* owner to make the accommodation available only for the summer season. This is because he can obtain maximum revenue for the least inconvenience. Rental prices in winter are barely half of what is demanded in July and August. A *gîte* may be part of a house – an annexe or a granny flat, for instance – that returns to regular use for the rest of the year.

LONG-TERM LETTING

Acts passed in 1986 and 1989 mean that a standard contract – *Contract de Location* – applies to all lettings of more than three months duration. This contract clearly sets out all the rights and responsibilities of landlord and tenant. A copy and translation of this contract is included in the appendices.

The lease

Landlord and tenant are required to hold copies of the contract. This document includes 12 key clauses:

◆ The letting period and commencement date.

◆ A description of the premises.

◆ The identification of common or shared parts of the building.

◆ The rental terms and payment intervals.

◆ A record of guarantee deposits, which must not be more than the sum of two month's rental.

◆ The proportion of service changes and local rates payable by landlord and tenant.

◆ The amount of tax payable on leasing. This is called *le droit de bail*.

◆ The responsibilities of landlord and tenant for maintenance and repair.

◆ Limitations applied to the use of the building.

◆ An inventory of fixtures and fittings.

◆ Penalty clauses relating to non-payment of rent.

◆ Conditions and consents required for sub-letting.

If the property is co-owned, additional information is contained in a separate document, *Le Reglement de Copropriete*, which sets out any special terms and conditions.

Legal protection of the tenant
French law is said to favour the tenant over the landlord. Many aspects of the lease confirm this view.

◆ The costs of setting up the lease agreement must be shared between landlord and tenant.

- If the lease contains a rent review clause it can only be exercised once annually.

- Any changes in the rent charged cannot be greater than the government's Cost of Construction Index figure.

- Disputed claims about responsibility for maintenance and repairs can be referred to an independent bailiff – a *huissier*. His report will be accepted by the court. This generally means that a landlord is forced to carry out necessary repairs.

- The tenant will have security of tenure for a minimum of 36 months. The only exception is a provision for repossession for 'family' or 'professional' reasons. Courts take a dim view of landlords who try to apply this clause unfairly.

- The tenant is required only to give three months notice. In the case of a person becoming unemployed or finding a new job, the requirement is only one month.

- If the landlord requires vacant possession he must inform the tenant in writing six months before the lease expires. If this does not occur it is assumed that the lease will be further renewed for a minimum period of 36 months.

- The tenant cannot be required to pay his rent by direct debit.

- The tenant cannot be required to make the property available for inspection at the weekend. Inspections must be of no more than two hours.

◆ The lease may have penalty clauses applied to non-payment of rent or service charges, but not for the breach of any other obligation.

INSTALMENT PURCHASE

A peculiarly French arrangement, which allows you to rent property while also buying some of the equity value is called *Location-Vente*. There are no parallels in English property transactions, though some housing associations are now encouraging a similar type of shared equity scheme. There are two methods of *location vente*:

Promesse unilaterale de vente

The vendor company lets a house or apartment in the normal way, but included with the lease is a promise to sell – the *promesse unilaterale de vente*. The tenant pays a higher rent than usual, which includes an element towards an agreed purchase price. An initial time period is fixed. This is generally two or three years.

This method is traditionally offered by property developers during slump periods. The main advantage to the tenant is that it allows him fully to assess the property before purchase. It is invariably cheaper than paying a substantial mortgage.

The disadvantage is that the tenant is only likely to acquire a small equity (between 3% and 5%) during the contract term. If he then decides to buy, this amount is, in effect, deducted from the purchase price. If he decides against buying, he loses the money he has paid.

Perhaps this is best seen as a letting arrangement dressed up as a purchase. It is generally not recommended.

Achat en viager

By this method the purchaser pays a substantial 'rent' for an indeterminate period of time before acquiring the property.

Again two contracts are combined. One of these is for a sale, and the other sets up a life annuity with the vendor as named beneficiary. This annuity is the *achat en viager*.

When the sales contract is drawn up the property is valued. The annuity is determined on actuarial (insurance) scales according to the vendor's life expectancy. The greater the expectancy, the lower the annuity payments will be.

This method is employed by specialist lawyers whose clients are elderly, and have no dependant relatives or children.

Entering into any contract of this type is, in essence, a gamble. The purchaser is effectively paying an income to the vendor (or vendors) in exchange for inheritance rights.

TIMESHARE

Bi-propriété

While the semi-detached house is a largely British institution, bi-propriété is characteristically French.

The French own more second homes pro rata than any other nation in Europe, but the bi-propriété boom began to decline a generation ago. Its popularity was based on a simple financial formula that provided substantial holiday residences for large families. Typically two senior family members (often brothers) would buy a seaside or country house and share the use of it.

The right to enjoy the property was technically divided over two six-month periods. The responsibilites of each share-holder (co-owner) were set out in contract.

The arrangement worked well in most cases through family cooperation and informal flexibility. During the summer months extended family groups would often meet under the shared roof. Half shares in the property were generally passed on from one generation to the next.

Bi-propriété is now a rarity. Smaller family units are more independent and they require less spacious accommodation. The second home is now more likely to be a seaside apartment or condominium – rather less suitable for a bi-propriété.

A legacy of difficulties created when shares in the property were passed beyond the family. The share value of one half of the bi-propriété is generally worth only about 40% of the whole.

Multi-propriété

What we know as timeshare the French call *multi-propriéte*. Although we may regard it as a long-term rental agreement, the word *propriété* means ownership.

This is stressed by marketing men. They also use such terms as *inter-proprété, poly-propriété,* and *pluri-propriété,* and increasingly you will hear *multi-propriété* called *multi-vacances* (literally many holidays) in order to encourge an impression of the recreational nature of the purchase.

Timeshare has not enjoyed a good press, and the variety of terms used to describe it begins to explain why. Even France's finest legal minds have become confused about the legal status of some timeshare agreements.

The difficulty arises because of what is actually bought. All timeshare owners purchase a *jouissance* – a right to occupy and enjoy property at designated times. Others (mainly since 1986) have also become part of a *société civile* – a company that holds voting shares in the property. This is intended to give them a say in the way the property is managed. In practice, though, as timeshare 'owners' are often scattered around a dozen countries, the management function is generally performed by an agent whose decisions may be arbitrary.

Timeshare purchasers now have rather more rights, but confusion in legal terminology means that some of them have also acquired more responsibilities. This partly explains why few pre-1986 purchasers have opted to form a *société civile.*

Multi-propriété has its aficionados who claim it is a way of enjoying a holiday home at a modest price.

Before purchasing timeshare ask yourself the following questions:

◆ How much does the timeshare really cost? Budget annually, and remember to count service, maintenance and administration charges. Compare this figure to the rental of a comparable *gîte* for the same time period. It can be argued that holiday rental is better value and timeshare can be perceived as an expensive way of paying for holidays in advance.

◆ Is the purchase a good investment? Marketing leaflets are likely to make this claim but many owners have lost money on re-sale. Pledges from timeshare companies to 'buy back' at market price should be treated with suspicion as timeshare resale brokers sell at a fraction of the original cost. It is even sometimes possible to acquire a 'free' timeshare by taking over the existing owner's maintenance contract.

◆ What procedures are there for resolving disputes? Any multi-occupied building has potential problems. Timeshare, by its very nature, has more potential users than most.

◆ What rights do you have to sub-let, or to re-assign your rights to others? Problems can occur with inherited timeshares, especially when there has been more than one signatory to an agreement.

◆ What are the arrangements for the maintenance of the building? Where timeshare purchasers are designated as co-owners the ultimate responsibility is theirs. A poorly maintained building will lose value and is more likely to be subject to vandalism.

◆ Are carpets, curtains, fixtures and fittings replaced systematically and regularly? There is evidence to suggest that equipment in multi-occupied apartments will wear out three times as quickly as usual.

4

Settling in France

INITIAL DOCUMENTATION

Although EU regulations have reduced the amount of documentation required for long stay visitors to member countries there are still a number of requirements in force.

Passport

A standard EU passport is valid for ten years. No visa is required for tourists staying in France for up to three months. A person who stays for longer than three months is classified as a resident.

Carte de sejour

The visa de longue durée (long stay visa) no longer exists although it is still regularly referred to, even by officials. It has been superseded by the *Carte de séjour de ressortissant de l'Union Europeenne* (EU resident permit). If you intend to become resident in France you have three months from entering the country to apply for your EU '*Carte de séjour*'.

You will require:

◆ A valid passport and three further passport photographs.

◆ Proof that you have residential accommodation.

◆ Proof that you pay into the French Social Security scheme.

◆ Proof of means of support. In practice this means either a contract of employment, or evidence of self-employment (from the local Chamber of Commerce), or evidence of a state pension or other recognised pension.

◆ Birth and marriage certificates.

If you are staying for a 'limited duration', a resident permit will be issued for this period of time, after which you will be re-assessed. If you are planning to stay on a 'permanent' basis, a resident permit will be issued for five years. After five years your permit can normally be renewed for a further ten years (and so on). And, according to the guidelines (www.ambafrance-uk.org) this '*right of residence granted by the permit) can be extended to the permit holder's spouse, dependant descendants (under 21) dependant ascendants and the spouse's ascendants*'.

French citizenship

Long-term residents sometimes choose to take French citizenship because foreigners are subject to an increasingly heavy burden of personal taxation. It is also possible, even prudent, to take the view that if you are to benefit from the French health and welfare systems it is better to be working towards French citizenship. You are required to:

◆ have lived in France for at least five years. For the spouses of people who already hold French citizenship and their children this regulation does not apply.

◆ be more than 18 years of age.

◆ have no criminal record.

◆ prove that you can speak and write in French to a reasonable standard.

MANAGING THE REMOVAL

Moving within the UK can be a stressful experience. Taking your property to France can be doubly so. A DIY removal is not recommended. Larger UK companies have a great deal of experience of the process. Although employing this expertise can be pricey, it is nevertheless recommended.

Import regulations

Household goods and personal effects can normally be imported into France duty free. Nevertheless there are a number of regulations, the breach of any of which can create considerable delay.

◆ Firearms may not be imported unless a special application has been processed. Details are available from consulates.

◆ A full inventory of goods (three copies) should be presented to officers when the first goods are taken to France. Property can then be imported in 'lots' but there is a time limitation (before import tax is imposed) of 12 months.

◆ Goods should correspond to the financial status of the owner. Customs will be suspicious of someone with a modest declared income importing a valuable collection of antiques. It is prudent to provide some form of proof of purchase for items of exceptional value.

◆ You will require a change of residence certificate from the *mairie* of the district you are moving to.

◆ A declaration of non-cession (non-transfer) is required. This is a statement that your household goods come within the duty free regulations.

◆ If your French property is to be used essentially as a holiday home or secondary residence additional rules apply.

It is these last rules that most frequently cause difficulty. Basically they state that all goods must have been owned and used by the importer for three months before the removal date and that they should be appropriate for usage in a secondary residence. The French would naturally prefer you to buy your goods in their country and they have been known to discourage imports. As most furniture and electrical goods are cheaper in the UK there is a natural temptation to take in as much as you can.

The best way to avoid problems is make purchases four to six months before export and keep their receipts. Electrical goods, especially if presented to customes in original packing, are most likely to provoke comment.

PETS

Since the pilot scheme was introduced in 2000, it has been possible to transport pets within the EU (and more recently the US and Canada) providing they fulfil the regulations. Briefly these are:

◆ Each animal must be micro chipped to meet agreed EU standards.

◆ The animal must have had an anti-rabies injection and blood tests must show the antibodies in the animal's blood.

◆ Six months must have elapsed from the successful blood test to the date of departure.

Initial costs will be about €350 per animal and then a further anti-rabies injection must be given bi-annually.

Animals that have successfully fulfilled the above obligations can then be taken to France through approved ports of embarkation and disembarkation. At the time of writing these were not all the Channel ports, but this is expected to change as usage of the scheme grows.

Those wishing to return to the UK with their pets must visit a French vet between 24 and 48 hours before departure to have the animal treated for ticks and fleas, and the relevant documents completed. This typically costs around €30.

Rules on animal imports are likely to change at short notice. DEFRA has a special PETS help line (☎ 0870 241 1710), or visit the website at www.defra.gov.uk.

Presently you are allowed to import up to three domestic animals into France, but only one of them may be a puppy or an animal under six months old. The date at which a French vaccination certificate is required is 12 months from the issue of the UK equivalent, and not, as is popularly thought, 12 months after the animal is imported to France.

French law requires dogs to have annual anti-rabies vaccinations. The number of the certificate must be tattooed into the dog's ear. British regulations have been amended to cover dogs that have been tattooed, then micro chipped and have the relevant vaccine certificates. These animals can then be re-imported to Britain.

HEALTHCARE

Your requirements will depend on the amount of time you intend to spend in France. Visitors who intend to stay for up to 12 months are covered by EU reciprocal arrangements with the UK.

For periods of up to 12 months you are theoretically covered by the E111 scheme. The form, which is available from your post office, must be filled in, signed, and stamped at the counter. The post office will retain a copy.

The E111 entitles you to go to any doctor or dentist in France who is a member of the state healthcare scheme. The form should last indefinitely, but a new one is required after each claim. Form E111 also entitles you to emergency hospital treatment. British consulates retain lists of English-speaking doctors.

Some medical practitioners take a photocopy of E111 and reclaim their fees from the reciprocal scheme but you may still have to pay up to 25% of the cost at the time. You may, however, be charged for the full cost of treatment. The silver lining is that, either way, E111 entitles you to reclaim at least most of these charges later. But it is worth noting:

◆ The claim is best made before returning to the UK, and as soon as possible after the treatment date.

◆ You will have to provide receipts for treatments and medicines, and apply to the local sickness insurance fund. The address will be listed in the T2 booklet issued with E111.

◆ You can apply for compensation in the UK. One problem with this is that fund administrators have been known to apply time limits to claims. If you require treatment and do not have an E111, one can be sent to you by getting in touch with Newcastle Benefits Directorate (☎ 0191 225 5811).

Medicines

Short stay visitors (those who have not applied for a *carte de séjour*) should take an adequate supply of regularly required medication with them. Each medicine should be labelled with both its generic and trade name and dosages should be clearly indicated.

NHS doctors are encouraged to supply only limited quantities of medicines. If you intend to be out of the UK for more than a month you will need certificate E112 to get further supplies in France. Enclose a covering letter from your doctor and write to:

Department of Health
Overseas Branch
Richmond House
79 Whitehall
London SW1A 2NL
☎ 020 7210 4850

Some pharmaceutical products are marketed in France with different brand names and others are formulated slightly differently. In some cases (particularly for patients suffering from a heart condition) it is best to arrange for an imported supply of medication. Doctors can give long-term prescriptions to UK pharmacists who can arrange for dispatch in sealed packaging together with the appropriate customs declarations. You should expect to pay around an extra €3 per package in addition to normal prescription charges.

It is worth remembering that French pharmacists, like their English counterparts, offer good advice on simple medicines like pain killers, mosquito repellents or those offering relief from cold symptoms.

Mail delivery times between France and the UK are notoriously irregular. It may be wise to retain several days emergency supply of regularly used medication.

Dental and eye care

French dentists and opticians are among the best qualified in Europe.

Replacing spectacles and contact lenses is straightforward if you have a copy of your prescription. Failing that, a phone call or email to the UK can quickly remedy the situation. A new eye test will automatically be carried out if the prescription is more than five years old (three years for those over 70 years of age).

There is a special 'dial a dentist' service for emergency home treatment, and for those staying in temporary accomodation. Charges are made and reclaimed in the same way as for other medical services.

HEALTHCARE FOR RESIDENTS

If you become resident in France you can choose to make voluntary contributions to the *Securité Sociale* which administers the French Health Service. If you are retired (and in receipt of the UK state pension) you are theoretically entitled to healthcare without making a contribution. Form E121 is required to prove this entitlement. Residents, whether retired or not, should seek a more permanent solution. This will inevitably include top up health insurance.

Choosing a doctor

As in the UK you are theoretically entitled to choose your own medical practitioner. In practice this may also mean registering at a local health centre or clinic.

However, French doctors are more likely than their UK counterparts to be working independently. Some are similar to our GPs, but the majority offer an additional specialist qualification. This specialist work is the most lucrative so French practitioners make a concerted effort to promote this area of their work. Choosing a doctor is therefore not as straightforward as in the UK. *Yellow Pages* may help, but personal recommendation is better.

Take family documentation to the *Relations Internationales* department of the Securité Sociale. This should include passports and marriage certificates including translations.

The *Relations Internationales* department is unable to recommend any individual doctor or practice. It does, however, provide information about many aspects of healthcare, and it holds lists of practitioners together with their specialisms.

Medical insurance

The French private health scheme is called the *mutuelle*. By joining you can reclaim any payment you have made for medical charges. In effect you are claiming back from the Health Service the difference of about 25% of total treatment charges that you have had to find from your own pocket. In certain circumstances (such as disability) it is possible to claim a supplementary or top up pension.

Again the *Relations Internationales* department will be able to explain the rules to you.

The French *Securité Sociale* is a network of organisations that provide welfare benefits. These are more extensive than their UK equivalents. To join the scheme is expensive, so private medical insurance is well worth considering. This is often cheapest and simplest to arrange in the UK. However, insurers may question a claim made from France unless you make your intentions clear on the proposal form. It is also worth checking the wording of the policy for limitations and exclusions sometimes applied to extended illnesses and chronic medical problems.

SAFEGUARDING YOUR PENSION

If you wish to safeguard your British pension rights, you are advised to continue to pay National Insurance contributions in the UK. It is possible to pay them while living abroad. Contact:

International Services
Inland Revenue National Insurance Contributions Office
Longbenton
Newcastle-upon-Tyne
NE98 1ZZ
☎ 0191 225 5811

EDUCATION

Although the French education system has become one of the most widely respected in Europe, many overseas residents choose to leave their youngsters in school on the UK mainland or elsewhere.

The alternatives

◆ a French public school.

◆ a French private school.

◆ an English-speaking private school.

◆ a bi-lingual school.

'Public' means a 'state' school in France. This may be considered as a good option for younger children. Studies have shown that most youngsters under eight years of age acquire a competence in the language within three months and near fluency within six. At age 11 competence comes within six months but near fluency can take a year. The clear message is that the age of the child is a key factor in his ability to adapt to the medium of a new language.

Private education is less common than in the UK, and these establishments often reflect the best and the worst in educational standards. Most of these schools are state aided and are found in the traditionally Catholic parts of the country – principally the Auvergne, Brittany and Savoie. Parents considering this option should take advice and inspect the school themselves.

There are very few English-speaking private schools. The reputable ones have high standards and competition for places is fierce. There are also a few bi-lingual schools. The best ones are large, successful, and based in the capital. Again there is heavy competition for places.

In rural areas parents are more likely to find state schools willing to take English-speaking youngsters. Public schools are not obliged to take anyone who cannot demonstrate reasonable standards of spoken and written French.

The system

Education throughout France is notionally free, but students have to buy their own textbooks and stationery. Emphasis is on hard work, the growth of personal responsibility and fierce competition.

The system begins at three years of age at an *école maternelle* (nursery). This is followed by the *école primaire* (primary school) and the *college d'enseignment secondaire* (CES). The best pupils are selected from the CES to attend a *lycée* which leads to the internationally recognised *baccalaureate* standard. The *'bac'* is the entrance ticket to university and higher education. Beyond this the grandes écoles (post graduate study centres) offer the route to the professions and in the upper reaches of the civil service.

Bursaries and grants are available for higher education, but these are normally paid in the form of scholarships to needy or exceptionally gifted youngsters. French law obliges parents to leave these gifted youngsters in the education system until they have reached their 20th birthday.

The different ethos of French schools can be summarised by the attitude to truancy. In France this is a serious offence that can lead to expulsion for the child and hefty fines for the parents. It is worth noting that teachers in France have greater status in the public eye than their UK counterparts.

Useful addresses

French Embassy Cultural Section
23 Cromwell Road
London
SW7 2EL
☎ 020 7838 2055 (general advice)

Service National d'Accueil aux Etudiants Etrangers
69 Quai D'Orsay
75007 Paris
(all aspects of student life, particularly those relating to higher education)

Service d'Information des Familles
277 Rue St Jacques
75005 Paris
☎ 01 43 29 12 77
(School directories and general guidance)

Centre National de Documentation sur L'Ensseignment
    Prive
20 Rue Faubert
75007 Paris
☎ 01 47 05 32 68

UTILITIES

Electricity

The French 220 volt/50 hertz supply is comparable to that of the UK and it is almost exclusively supplied by *Elecricité de France* (EDF). French electricity is possibly the cheapest in Europe and standards of installation, particularly for new property, are satisfactory.

But there are problems. Some older buildings still use the 110/120 volt AC supply which requires a transformer to convert the supply to 220 volts AC for motorised appliances. If the wattage available from the transformer is less than the rating of the appliances they will not work – or at least not at the same time. More bizarrely the level of supply, even for 220 volts AC, will depend on the kilowatt (kw) supply you have metered by EDF. This agreed supply level, which can vary from 3kw to 36kw, is a significant part of the standing charge equation with the maximum supply costing about 40% more than the minimum. Small to medium-size households usually operate on a 6kw supply with a device known as a *delesteur* – which cuts out 'supplementary systems' (such as convectors and water heaters) when high-consumption appliances (such as washing machines and electric kettles) threaten to overload the system.

Older rural properties may not have an electricity supply and paying to have it connected to the grid can be prohibitively expensive. This is particularly true if the property is within a national park where only underground supplies are permitted. EDF will quote for the work but alternatives, including generators and solar energy, may be more economically viable. It is worth noting in this context that the cost of rewiring a three bedroom property is likely to be around €4,400.

Even where 220AC is supplied rural areas, in particular, suffer regular power cuts. This is most likely to be as a result of a generation or system failure, but could also be a consequence of industrial action. Happily, most interruptions are only momentary but are sufficient to knock out some timing devices and to crash computers. Specification for computer systems in France therefore invariably includes an un-interrupted power supply (UPS) with battery back-up.

The price for electricity depends on the tariff option you choose. Leaflets explaining the alternatives are issued when each new installation is made and when a new customer account is opened. They are also available on demand from any EDF office.

They amount to either:

◆ The Blue Tariff. This is either the normal tariff (option base) where charges remain constant throughout the 24-hour cycle, or the reduced rate (*option heures creuses*) where up to three periods (totalling a maximum eight hours a day) are earmarked for lower cost supply. The *option base* is selected by owners of properties that are only occasionally occupied. The reduced rate option, which features a two dial metre that records both 'normal' and 'off peak' usage, is the rate most commonly applied.

◆ The Tempo Tariff (*option tempo*). This increasingly popular tariff is designed to encourage fuel saving at times when demand is at its greatest. It provides the customer with cheap off-peak electricity for most of the year. There are, however, some variations from this – the most significant being some 22 peak days (falling between 1 November and 31 March) which are determined by EDF by reference to the meteorological centre in Toulouse. At these peak periods the tariff charged is up to eight times the off-peak period. Peak days are announced by a light or buzzer. The *tempo* tariff, which also has a lower standing charge, can only be applied to homes where the power supply is rated at nine or more kw and there must also be a viable alternative (non-electrical) source of heat. Those who choose the *tempo* tariff normally have a remote controller which switches off high consumption appliances during the peak periods. This tariff is particularly suitable for people who have a property that is unoccupied during the winter or for those with homes on the Mediterranean coast.

Under French law any new building or flat can be joined to the mains system. The developer has the responsibility of making sure that a building conforms to the regulations and that the appropriate certificate (*certificate de conformité*) is issued for new property. This is handed over to EDF.

A deposit is required which is refunded in portions after five and ten years. A second nominal charge is made for the meter when it is connected to the supply. In some circumstances a bond is required that can be set against future electricity bills.

Though supplies and installations may be cheap, some safety standards are not what we have come to expect in the UK. Watch out for:

◆ Insufficient power points, particularly in the kitchen. This is a chronic problem which seems peculiar to France within Europe. It even extends to the most recently developed property where you will still find up to half a dozen low wattage appliances run from a multi-plug connector fed from a single socket.

◆ Unearthed electrical equipment. Dishwashers, driers, washing machines, and televisions are normally earthed. Special sockets are fitted to hobs, cookers and ovens.

◆ Timed earth trips. You sometimes have to wait several minutes after replacing a fuse before the normal supply is restored.

◆ Insecure light fittings and loose wall sockets with both bayonet and screw light fittings in the same room and sometimes even on the same wall.

◆ Some imported electrical equipment which is not compatible with the French 220 volt/50 cycle system, or not fitted with a slow start system. The power surge produced by turning on an imported electric kettle or microwave is often sufficient to blow the fuses or trip-switches.

◆ A multitude of plug and socket fittings, some unearthed, and almost all without fuses.

Gas

Gas in France is either town gas or bottled gas. Town gas is generally available in more densely populated urban areas and not at all in the countryside. It is supplied by state-owned Gaz de France (GDF).

If you buy a town property and wish to have it connected the charge is a little under €800 provided you are within 35 metres of the nearest supply point. There are four tariff options based on the number of cubic metres you are likely to use. This is calculated on the basis of factors such as whether or not gas is to be used for cooking, hot water and central heating. As in the UK (since 1992) the amount you actually use is converted into kilowatt hours for billing. Where gas is only used for cooking in shared buildings, the bills are paid by the *co-propriété* and added to individual service charges.

As electricity is relatively cheap, visitors are often surprised to learn that most French homes have a back up (usually bottled) gas supply. Additionally there will often be a second (gas) hob fitted in the kitchen near to the electric one. This is because electricity supplies are so regularly interrupted. Bottled gas is available at most garages and supermarkets. As in the UK you are required to pay a container deposit. Propane is considered to be a better option than butane. Although slightly less efficient it is less affected by cold weather. In some rural areas it is possible to install garden based gas tanks from companies such as Antargaz and Total. These are normally fitted free of charge in exchange for a supply contract of one year or more. One downside of this arrangement is an increase in insurance premiums.

Water

French water is the most expensive in the world – typically around 60% higher than in the UK. Unlike the state monopolies of electricity and gas, all French water is supplied by private companies. The largest of these – Cise, Lyonnaise des Eaux, Saur and Vivendi – supply 80% of the market. If you have a septic tank the bill will be reduced by up to 40%. Special rates apply for industrial and agricultural use, and for swimming pools.

Water supplies are metered. The metres are reliable and it is therefore difficult to question charges, which vary from €2 to €5 per cubic metre (1,000 litres) depending on location. The psychological effect of metering, explains why in France you will rarely see a domestic sprinkler system or hosepipe in operation.

Supply shortages are rare in urban areas but common in rural areas during the summer. When water levels run low the supply is simply turned off. Many rural homes have an emergency storage tank and keep grey (recycled house) water for the garden.

In central and southern France a significant number of properties are supplied by spring water or wells. The water is usually of excellent quality, and, best of all, virtually free.

Telephones (PTT)

Applications for a telephone are made to the local Agence Commerciale des Télécommunications. Installations have been known to take place the following day but delays of up to 12 months are not unknown.

Those used to the UK's standard installation system are sometimes shocked by charges levied in France. Connections within a block of flats are inexpensive, but if your new home is several miles from existing connections the charge will reflect the work involved.

The standard connection is called the *ligne mixte* This is not a party line, but one that allows calls to be made in and out.

It is also worth noting:

♦ Ex-directory numbers are subject to a monthly surcharge.

♦ There are two phone books for each *département* – the *annuaire* (domestic listings) and the *professions* (Yellow Pages). The *annuaire* lists subscribers under towns and communes. The *professions* contains business listings and all those useful numbers that UK subscribers are used to finding in their standard phonebook.

♦ Lines may go silent between phases of dialling a number, and the ringing tone is frequently inaudible.

Those used to the relative efficiency of BT may find its French equivalent – France Telecom – a source of frustration. Lines, particularly into the capital, are overloaded and regularly unavailable during office hours. PTT Directory Enquiries has a poor record of giving correct numbers and checking overseas listings is often beyond them.

Mobile phones
Mobile phone coverage in France is excellent. This partly

because networks share cells and partly because those living in the regions demand parity with Paris. You can generally log on to a network at the top of an Alp or at the bottom of a gorge. In military training areas, however, service can be suspended from time to time.

UK bought mobiles theoretically work in France. Whether or not they do in practice depends on your SIM card and contract. Advance line rental and monthly line rental contracts usually allow international roaming. 'Pay As You Talk' arrangements may not. Check with your service provider before you leave the UK. Do not assume that international roaming has been automatically enabled. The same applies to mobile fax and data services. Networks do their best to ration new numbers.

Using your UK mobile in France is expensive – particularly between 0700 and 1900. Even off-peak calls rapidly add up and text messages can cost as much as €1 each and calls made to your mobile appear on your bill. France Telecom bills your network provider who adds a second round of supplementary charges and VAT before billing you. Some UK network providers – such as Vodaphone – even pro-gramme their handsets to locate automatically the overseas providers with whom they have negotiated a mutually bene-ficial agreement. You can, however, search for alternative providers.

Generally, however, a more economical option is tempor-arily to exchange your Sim card for its French equivalent although in so doing your mobile will temporarily lose its UK identity. It is therefore not at all uncommon now for UK mobiles to have a daytime French identity before reverting to the Rule Britannia around sunset.

THE MEDIA

The French media is generally more serious minded than in the UK. Nowhere is this more true than in television.

Television

There are six network channels in France with up to 24-hour broadcasting. Two channels are state controlled, and the others are monitored by an official watchdog organisation which has the power to revoke their licences.

The formula is similar to the UK with a large number of quiz shows, sit-coms, movies and news programmes. The French do not share the British addiction to soaps, but they enjoy comedy and variety. There is more arts programming and a great deal of political debate and discussion.

Along parts of the northern coast and up to 20 miles inland it is possible to receive UK terrestrial signals although in sheltered positions a signal booster is required. The French TV SECAM system is incompatible with the UK PAL standard. Duel standard TV sets – such as those manufactured by Roadstar – are available. Conversions are possible but equally expensive. It is generally cheaper and easier to buy a new set, unless you plan to rely entirely on satellite transmissions.

Satellites beam down hundreds of English language channels around 20 of which are available on a free-to-view basis.

Following the BBC's withdrawal (May 2003) from the Sky platform their channels (including audio) can only be received in a smaller 'footprint' (optimum reception area), which means that reception of these channels will depend on location. ITV is reviewing its plans for satellite broadcasting.

France is at the heart of the 'footprint' for channels carried on the Sky platform. The quality of reception – even with a small 20cm dish – is excellent although from the Massif Central southwards it may be necessary to tune in to Sky Digital Southern Europe. This is achieved through accessing the System Set Up menu via your remote control. Following the changeover do not be alarmed if there are some glitches in automatic translation to wide-screen format.

Radio

Radio reception is generally excellent in France.

The main stations are:

France Culture – Concerned with the arts and literature
France Inter – Mainly current events and discussions
France Musique – Mainly classical music and jazz

There are dozens of FM commercial stations offering pop, easy listening, sport and news updates.

BBC for Europe (MW 648 khz/463 m) transmits around the clock with most daytime programmes in English. Radio 1, Radio 2 and Radio 5 can be picked up close to the northern coast. Radio 4 reception on Long Wave is adequate as far south as the Loire valley. BBC World Service is available almost everywhere. There are presently no plans to make UK digital stations available in France, but the Sky platform allows you to receive some of them via your television. There is also the possibility of listening to programmes on the internet.

Newspapers

The most widely distributed newspapers are:

L'Equipe – Very successful daily paper. Emphasis on sport
Le Figaro – Right of centre quality daily
France-Soir – Similar to UK tabloids in approach and content
Le Monde – Independent left of centre quality daily.

English newspapers are widely distributed in France, especially during the holiday season. South of the channel ports and Paris you are most likely to see yesterday's newsprint on the stands.

A number of UK papers can appear in a modified (reduced) format. One of these is the *Continental Daily Mail*. Others, like the *Guardian Weekly*, are special editions prepared for the European market.

MOTORING

It is said that the character of the French people changes once they climb into the driving seat. It is also claimed that behaviour on the open road varies only between the intolerant and the homicidal. In Europe only the Belgians have a worse reputation for recklessness behind the wheel.

Younger French women are as aggressive as their male counterparts and the one fingered salute invariably punctuates a dangerous overtaking manoeuvre. In Paris the motorcar is used as a battering ram to create a parking space. Indeed the Paris '75' registration plate is seen as a warning beacon to those who regard hospitalisation as an unsatisfactory outcome to a journey.

The French adore their fast cars as much as they despise cleaning them. Speed is a matter of national pride. While the UK blundered along with decrepit and unreliable railways and rolling stock the French created the TGV – the fastest and most efficient railway in the world. In doing so they swept aside the objections of farmers and vineyard owners but accepted a six-month delay in track laying because of a nest of eagles!

For the French it is debatable as to whether the vote or the motorcar is the true cornerstone of democracy. Potential French drivers have to pass the most rigorous written and practical tests before they are granted a licence. The licence itself is a status symbol which once earned appears to allow an almost complete disregard for the rules of the road. While the UK employs more speed cameras than traffic police the French regard a battle of wits with motorcycle traffic police as a game. Flashing headlights during daylight are often a warning of a mobile radar trap. Speed cameras remain a political hot potato.

The driver and the law

◆ You have to be over 18 with a full licence to drive in France.

◆ The French drive on the right.

◆ It is a legal requirement to carry a red warning triangle and a spare set of light bulbs.

◆ Third-party insurance is compulsory.

◆ Driving documents, including your licence and vehicle registration document must be available for inspection.

You are advised to carry a *constat* – a specially printed form to be filled in immediately after an accident. This can prevent difficulties with insurance claims, especially if there is hidden damage to your vehicle.

French roads are designated as motorways (A for *autoroute*), *routes nationales* (N roads, rather like our 'A' roads) and *routes departmentales* (D roads). Most motorways are toll roads with a speed limit of 130kph. 110kph is the norm for dual carriageways, 90kph for single carriageways, and 60kph in urban areas. Routes nationales are frequently much less busy than their British equivalents.

Speed limits are rigorously enforced by traffic police. Toll cards are time stamped and there are both radar and camera speed traps. For minor offences (*contraventions*) police can impose a fixed penalty fine (*amende forfaitaire*).

This fixed penalty scheme includes:

◆ Not using seat belts, carrying a child under ten in the front seat, illegal use of the horn and causing an obstruction – all about €20.

◆ Dangerous parking or parking at a bus stop, careless driving, ignoring signs and priority rules, speeding, and failing to stop at a traffic light – all about €140.

Failure to pay fixed penalty fines within 30 days means the offence is reclassified as *une amende majorée*. These are dealt with through the courts and fine levels are increased by 120%.

The legal limit for drinking and driving is the same as in the UK and the law is applied in much the same way. The French penalty system is ruthless. Despite this severity French driving behaviour, especially in busy towns, can create the impression that there is no law and accident statistics during peak holiday periods make horrific reading.

Driving licence

The British driving licence used to be valid in France for 12 months after which you were required to apply for a French one. However, an EU Driving Licence Directive now requires the mutual recognition of all driving licences issued within the EU.

In theory this means you will not require a French licence. However, since 1992, the French have operated a complex and controversial system in respect of motoring offences.

Holders of French licences begin with 12 points which are deducted according to the severity of offences. Deductions range from one point for failing to dip headlights to six for driving under the influence of alcohol. When all 12 points are lost you forfeit your licence. Points are normally re-instated three years after conviction. It is also much more common in France to have your licence temporarily suspended. These short suspensions are typically from seven to 28 days.

Those who are subject to a resident's permit and who also commit a motoring offence in France are required to obtain a French driving licence so that the points system can be applied to them. And, as the application process takes at least two months and the UK licence has to be surrendered with the application for the French one, you could find yourself in a legal minefield.

If you are likely to be spending more time in France than in the UK it is therefore recommended that you apply for a French licence as soon as you receive your resident's permit. To make the application you will require your UK licence with a translation, your resident's permit, proof of domicile and two passport photographs. The French issuing authority is the *Service du Permis de Conduire de la Préfecture de Police*.

Importing a vehicle

If you import your vehicle you will require French licence plates (*plaques d'immatriculation*) after six months. You apply to the *préfecture de police* who send you a number. A local garage will make up and fit the plate for a modest fee.

Vehicle owners are also required to obtain registration documents for the vehicle (the *carte grise*). A *carnet de passage en douanes* (certificate of passage through customs) is a further document to retain if you are considering importing the vehicle.

The carte grise
The French roadworthiness test is similar to the UK MOT.

The demands for testing are sent out by *departements* at different times of the year. For cars imported from the UK headlights will have to be realigned for the right hand side of the road. Passing the road-worthiness test secures you the *carte grise* – a document that must be produced when your insurance is renewed.

Duty
French residents (and temporary residents) who import their vehicles from the UK within 12 months can do so tax free.

There is no set limit on the number of vehicles that can be imported. The rule is that they must have been the personal property of the resident for six months prior to import and they cannot be sold for six months after the import date.

If you intend to import a vehicle you will require documentation from a French consulate in the UK.

Buying a vehicle in France
There are advantages to this:

◆ Vehicle values remain lower in France despite the UK's recent price reductions.

◆ For up to six months you can run the vehicle on temporary (TT) plates if you pay in foreign currency.

◆ Left-hand drive vehicles are safer to drive and easier to sell in France. There are some small, but significant parts for right-hand drive vehicles that are difficult, or impossible to obtain in France. Accelerator cables, for instance, are invariably a different length.

Vehicle insurance

In the short term you can extend your UK cover by asking your insurers for an international insurance certificate (green card). For this you may pay a modest supplementary premium or administration fee. Motor insurance for unlimited third-party liability is compulsory in France and premiums are relatively expensive because of the large number of accidents and stolen vehicles.

The French vehicle insurance market is also fairly complex. Progressively the policies on offer are:

Third party only. The legal minimum which covers the damage and medical costs sustained by a third party.

Third party, fire and theft. Adds cover against natural hazards – such as fire and rock falls – and the theft of the vehicle, its contents, and legal expenses.

Multi-risk. Adds cover for the damage done to your vehicle in the event of a collision with a vehicle or animal belonging to an identifiable person.

Comprehensive. Adds cover for damage to your vehicle if the third party cannot be identified.

Comprehensive with driver protection. While driver protection insurance – which adds cover for injury and incapacity – can be added to all the insurance options it is most commonly added to comprehensive cover.

Premiums are loaded against drivers under the age of 25 and those who have been convicted of drunken or dangerous driving. All vehicles worth more than €15,000 must have the registration number engraved on the windows and have an alarm fitted. Vehicles not securely garaged overnight are surcharged. No claims bonuses of up to a maximum 50% can be earned after ten years. UK earned bonuses can be transferred for up to this amount provided there is written evidence (not a renewal notice) from a UK insurer. If you hold the maximum bonus for three years one accident will not reduce it. Many French insurers also require a translation. Bonuses are cancelled if you do not hold vehicle insurance for a period of two years.

Claims, which must be submitted within five days of an incident, are generally dealt with on the basis of reports from the police and the drivers concerned. If you are judged to be less than 30% responsible your bonus will not be affected. Repairs are normally sanctioned by insurance assessors. When a vehicle is reported stolen the claim will not be considered for 30 days.

5

Financial matters

BANKING IN FRANCE

Even if you intend to live in France it is well worth considering retaining a British bank account – or at least until the UK embraces the euro. If nothing else, this will save the cost of currency exchange when visiting Britain.

Though it is theoretically possible for residents to manage without a French bank account, it is undoubtedly more convenient to have one. French banking rules are, however, rather different to those in most other EU countries. It is best to be aware of the way the system works.

The differences

Exchange controls were lifted in the UK some years ago which means you can take an unlimited amount of sterling into France. You are, however, only permitted to take €8,000 out of the country at any one time, although the Banque de

France has generally made an exception for foreigners who wish to export the net proceeds of a property sale.

Opening a bank account

Foreigners can open a special account called a *compte étranger* (literally a stranger's account). Sterling can be paid in by normal bank transfer methods, or by cheque or cash. The French government has sought to reduce tax evasion by discouraging 'cash' deals. This means that French notes and coinage cannot be paid into bank accounts.

The *compte étranger* can be an ordinary/current account (*compte cheques*) or a deposit account (*compte sur livret*). The ordinary account provides you with a cheque book, and the deposit account pays interest. Orders for new cheque books can take several weeks to process so it is best to keep a spare book.

Arrangements for statements are similar to those in force in the UK, but it is unwise to assume that your statement is up to date. There are good reasons why the French clearing system is referred to as *la tortue* – the tortoise.

When you open an account the bank will check with central records to find out if you are subject to an interdiction – a ban from holding a bank account. Inter-bank communication is excellent. A UK bankruptcy, a withdrawal of credit notice, or a court order for debt or non payment, will almost certainly prevent you from opening an ordinary account.

Interest

Gross interest is paid on deposit accounts. It is your

responsibility to declare this to the taxman either in France or the UK. The double taxation agreement between the countries means that you are only liable to pay tax once.

Most banks impose a minimum balance for ordinary accounts – usually around €100. Interest is not ordinarily paid on these accounts unless you agree to maintain a higher minimum balance.

Credits and debits

Cheques paid into your account are credited on the same day, even if post-dated, but you cannot draw against them until clearance is complete.

French cheques are similar to those in the UK with the amount written in both words and numbers. If the amounts are different the words will be assumed to be correct. Cheques must be endorsed. Open cheques will be honoured but this can lead to delay. Crossed cheques are recommended. Cheques can only be stopped for security reasons – this generally means notifying the bank that it has been lost or stolen.

Using – and misusing – your cheques

French law allows traders to refuse a cheque for any amount less than €15, and cash for any amount greater than that. Both events are rare. Indeed, as part of the continued battle against 'cash' deals, French law now insists that cheques are issued as payment for work or services valued at more than €150. The law has recently been extended to apply to rents and office supplies.

Cheque guarantee cards are not issued in France, but some form of proof of identity is likely to be required. French nationals carry identity cards.

The French are very tough on misuse of bank accounts. If you bounce a cheque the bank will instruct you to put matters right. If you fail to do so within the 30-day time limit your cheque book will be withdrawn, the account is frozen and you are subject to a ban (an interdiction). The ban is recorded with the Banque de France and the file is retained for two years during which time you may not open or operate a bank account in France. Even if your account is regularised within 30 days, a second offence within the year will incur a 12-month chequebook ban.

Financial penalties for bouncing cheques are severe. These can range from a fine of €450 to €40,000. Prison sentences of up to five years can be (and occasionally are) imposed. Misunderstanding the system, or claiming the problem arose through the slowness of the clearing system have not proved to be adequate defences in law.

UK banks in France
All the major UK banks are represented in France, although outside the major cities the branches are thinly distributed.

The advantage of dealing with a UK bank in France is primarily one of communication. Banks of all nationalities are subject to French banking law.

Bank dispensers and credit cards
Bank dispensers (*distributeurs*) are similar to those operating

in the UK, with the additional advantage that many offer an English language program for transactions. Many dispensers do not accept the older type of metallic strip card which are being replaced (as they expire) by 'chip and pin' – which are generally accepted. UK debit cards (such as 'Switch') are virtually useless in France.

Credit card companies monitor transactions in order to limit fraud. If a card, which has not been used outside the UK for some time, is suddenly used for cash withdrawals in France it may be 'flagged'. If your card is rejected by a number of French bank dispensers this is possibly the reason. Check with your credit card issuer, or, better still, inform them of time periods when you intend to use the card for cash withdrawals outside the UK.

For a modest fee French banks will issue a *carte de retrait* (withdrawal card). Much better (but pricier) is a *carte de paiement national* which allows withdrawals from any dispenser in the Carte Bancaire group which includes most of the major banks. Carte Bancaire dispensers are identified by the distinctive CB logo.

Dispensers can be found on high streets and at strategic points close to hypermarkets and shopping precincts.

The use of *le plastique* is now commonplace in France. Microchip cards ('chip and pin') are known as *cartes des puces* – literally flea cards. After paying at a cash desk, card owners are required to enter their 'pin' number into a hand-held machine to confirm the transaction. This system is now being introduced in the UK.

The Visa card is by far the most useful (as Visa is part of the Carte Bancaire group) but a larger number of points of sale are now accepting Mastercard. Some French traders (particularly supermarkets) will not accept credit cards or cheques for small amounts – usually less than €15. Traders must have a clear sign showing that this policy is in force.

American Express is accepted in up-market hotels, restaurants and stores. These are mainly found in the capital and larger towns and cities.

TAXATION
The basic taxes for individuals are:

◆ Income tax. This is divided in French law into earned income (*impot sur le revenue*) and unearned income (*impot des revenues des capitaux mobliers*).

◆ Land tax (*taxe fonciere*).

◆ Community tax (*taxe d'habitation*).

◆ Capital gains tax (*regime des plus-values des particuliers*).

◆ Death duties (*droits de succession*).

◆ Gift tax (*droits de donation*).

Registration
The ownership of all properties must be registered with the French tax authorities. Owners who are not resident have to register by 30 April following completion of the property purchase. Residents are expected to register immediately

with the local Centre des Impots. Non-resident owners should register with the Tax Centre for Non Residents at:

Centre des Impots des Non-residents
9 Rue D'Uzes
75094 Paris

Domicile

For international tax purposes the concept of domicile is important. Those who have their 'fiscal domicile' in one country theoretically pay tax in that country on their income. There is, however, some give and take on this. Some pensions, for instance, originating in the UK, are automatically taxed there.

Those considered to be domiciled outside France pay tax only on that portion of their income earned in France. You will be said to have a French fiscal domicile if:

◆ You have a home in France and spend more than 183 days in the country in any financial year.

◆ Your wife and family live in France for more than 183 days in any financial year, even if you spend most of your time out of the country.

◆ You work in France on either a salaried or self employed basis, unless you can prove that work is ancillary to your main employment.

◆ Most of your income is generated in France. This could for instance catch retired people who run a successful gîte business.

Income tax

If you are domiciled in France you are liable to pay income tax. The French tax laws are complex and there will be winners and losers in comparison with the UK system.

Long term residents frequently choose to take French citizenship because foreigners are subject to an increasingly heavy burden of personal taxation.

There is an outline of the system below. Detailed information is available from a French government inter-departmental economic agency – Délégation à l'Amenagement du Térritoire et a l'Action Régionale (DATAR). Their UK address is:

21–24 Grosvenor Place
London
SW1X 7HU
☎ 020 7823 1895

Essentially DATAR's UK office is intended to offer fiscal advice for anyone considering selling to the French market, or setting up a business in France itself. Their publications include helpful advice on personal taxation.

Their address in France is:

1 Avenue Charles Floquet
75007 Paris
☎ 01 47 83 61 20 or 01 40 65 12 34

French income tax is assessed on a family basis. The husband is responsible for the return which includes the income of his wife and children who are still in the educational system, or doing their military service. Divorced, separated or widowed persons claim allowances according to circumstances. Across the board allowances include:

◆ Money spent on major property repairs.

◆ Money spent on certain 'green projects' such as the installation of solar energy panels for heating.

◆ Payments for maintenance and dependent relatives other than children.

◆ Gifts to certain charities.

◆ Contributions to the Securité Sociale.

◆ Approved life assurance premiums.

◆ Interest payments on certain loans.

◆ Special arrangements for single parents with young children.

Taxable income is worked out by deducting allowances from total income and dividing the net figure by:

◆ One for a single person with no children.

◆ Two for a married couple with no children.

◆ 2.5 for a married couple with one child.

◆ An extra 0.5 for each additional child. A married couple with four children will divide by four.

When a taxable income has been worked out the rates that apply fall into a banded structure. The following are approximate figures for those incurring an incoming tax liability in France in 2002. They are based on indexing the tax authorities 2001 figures. The following bands should therefore be treated only as a rough guide:

The first €5,666 of taxable income is tax free
€5,666 to €6,166 – 5%
€6,166 to €7,000 – 10%
€7,001 to €10,833 – 15%
€10,834 to €14,000 – 20%
€14,001 to €18,333 – 25%
€18,334 to €21,333 – 30%
€21,334 to €25,334 – 35%
€25,334 to €41,000 – 40%
€41,001 to €58,000 – 45%
€58,001 to €67,166 – 50%
€67,167 to €77,333 – 55%
€77,334 and upwards – 58%

A married couple with no children, no allowances and a joint income of €41,666 would pay tax as follows:

Half of €41,666 is €20,833, so each has a taxable income of €20,833

On the first €5,666 no tax is paid
On the next €500 at 5 per cent €25
On the next €833 at 10 per cent €83
On the next €3,833 at 15 per cent €575
On the next €3,166 at 20 per cent €633

On the next €4,333 at 25 per cent €1,083
On the final €2,500 at 30 per cent €833
Total €3,233

Thus their joint tax bill would be (€3,233 x 2) €6,466

The same couple living in England would automatically have personal allowances of €7,384 each. Their tax bill would look like this:

Individual taxable income €20,833 – €7,384 = €13,499
Tax on first €3,072 @ 10% = €307

Tax on next €10,427 @ 22% = €2,294
Total = €2,601

Thus their joint tax bill would therefore be double €2,601 or €5,202.

The French tax system benefits large families and those on relatively low incomes. The tax year runs from 1 January each year and bills are paid in three equal instalments in the year following the liability.

Filling in a tax return is difficult because of the complexity of the system and the amount of technical language involved. English-speaking residents paying income tax in France invariably require the services of an accountant.

When the authorities suspect that tax declarations are inaccurate or fraudulent they will investigate. In certain circumstances residents with complex tax affairs (including perhaps income from a number of sources outside France) will be assessed according to the punitive *regime de d'imposition forfaiture.*

Using this system income is assessed according to arbitrary norms. This includes ascribing a letting value to all properties you own and multiplying it by a factor of three or five. Cars are valued and taxed at 75% of maximum new showroom value, servants are assumed to have massive salaries, and race horses are reckoned to be winners.

The system is rarely applied but it demonstrates what can happen to those who fall foul of the tax authorities.

Land tax
Taxe foncière is levied by the local commune and is very similar to the system of parish rates in the UK. Registers of all property and owners are maintained at the *mairie.*

Property is given a notational letting value on which the *taxe foncière* is based. Exceptions include government and public buildings, grain stores, wine presses and stables. New buildings are exempt from the tax for two years.

The last general valuation of buildings was carried out in 1974. The tax levied is adjusted annually in line with the index of inflation.

Community tax
Taxe d'inhabitation is paid by the resident occupier of a property on 1 January each year. It is calculated according

to the value of amenities. These include the size of the property, including garages, outbuildings and land. If the property is not subject to a lease, then the owner of the property is liable for the payment of the tax.

The base rate of the tax is calculated again on the notional letting value of the property, last calculated in 1987 and up rated since then by indexation.

This tax is reduced when the property is used as the pincipal residence of a family. Since 1989 each commune has fixed *taxe d'habitation* at rates of five, ten or 15% of the lettable value.

Both *taxe foncière* and *taxe d'habitation* are payable by UK residents whether or not the property is designated as their main residence. But even taken together they rarely amount to 65% of the average UK Council Tax Band D. In France it is national rather than local taxation that really hurts.

Capital gains tax

The *regime de plus value des particuliers* is imposed on anyone who is domiciled in France when assets are sold, but their primary residence is exempted. But the tax is invariably applied to those selling French property who are domiciled abroad.

The tax is levied at 33%. The capital gain is deemed to be the difference between purchase price and sale price, but the seller can offset:

◆ The supplementary costs of making the purchase, or 10% of the purchase price – whichever is the greater.

◆ An indexation of the increase in property values calculated according to government figures.

French law demands that foreign sellers employ an agent to handle the sale. This agent (normally a *notaire*) is respon-. sible for paying the tax to the government. It is possible to get clearance for payment before completion. This is highly recommended. It saves time and paperwork and will reduce the fee the agent charges for his services.

In practice the capital gains tax payable on a property sale is likely to be modest or non existent for many sellers. But those who improve property considerably, or create new residential units (such as an integral independent granny flat) are most likely to find themselves paying for the privilege. The tax is designed to catch foreigners who are systematically renovating French property for profit.

Inheritance tax

French law is very concerned with the idea of passing down assets within a family. The concept is called *patrimoine* and it is the guiding principle of *droits de succession*. The main elements of *patrimoine* are that:

◆ Payments are made by those who inherit, according to the value of assets they receive and their relationship to the deceased.

◆ All assets in France are subject to *droits de succession*.

- The assets of those domiciled in France include property at home and abroad.

- The assets of those not domiciled in France exclude property outside the country. Double tax agreements with other countries ensure that *droits de succession* paid in France is exempted from tax liability elsewhere.

The rates of inheritance tax given below are based on current bands.

- When an estate passes to a surviving spouse or a relative in direct ascendant or descendant line there is a tax-free allowance of €45,000 per beneficiary.

- After that a surviving spouse pays:

5% on the next €8,333
10% on amounts between €8,333 and €16,666
15% on amounts between €16,666 and €33,333
20% on amounts between €33,333 and €566,666
30% on amounts between €556,666 and €933,333
35% on amounts between €933,333 and €2,000,000
40% on amounts in excess of €2,000,000

- The ascendant or descendant relative pays:

5% on the next €8,333
10% on amounts between €8,333 and €12,500
15% on amounts between €12,500 and €15,666
20% on amounts between €15,666 and €566,666
25% on amounts between €566,666 and €933,333

30% on amounts between €933,333 and €2,000,000
40% on amounts in excess of €2,000,000

◆ Divorced or unmarried brothers and sisters have a beneficiary allowance of €16,666. The same allowance can be claimed if they are more than 50 years of age or suffer from infirmity. After this they pay:

35% on all amounts up to €2,500
45% on all amounts above €2,500

◆ Third degree relatives – aunts, uncles, nephews, nieces and cousins pay 55% of the inheritance received.

◆ Any other beneficiary (apart from certain charities) will pay a rate of 60%.

Gift tax

The rules for *droits de donation* are similar to those applied above. The idea is to prevent the avoidance of inheritance tax.

There is some mitigation for:

◆ Gifts given as wedding presents.

◆ Gifts made by people under the age of 65.

Value added tax

There are presently five rates of taxe sur la valeur ajoutée (TVA) in France:

◆ 5.5% for most agricultural and food products.

◆ 7% on travel, entertainment, catering, hotels, medicines and most books.

◆ A standard rate of 18.6% for most other items.

◆ 20.6% for some services.

◆ 33% on luxury goods, tobacco, and pornography. The French call this *taxe du pêche* – sin tax.

The sale of new properties (or any first sale within five years of construction) is subject to TVA. This will always be included in the sale price and will be paid by the developer.

Any property resold within that five-year period is also subject to TVA. This concerns UK buyers more than is necessary. The amount is not usually considerable because the seller offsets the amount paid in TVA on the initial sale, and French property values generally advance more cautiously than our own. Only when a property has been significantly improved or modified during the five-year period is it likely to attract a significant TVA bill.

WILLS AND INHERITANCE

Le testament is an important document for all those considering entering the French property market.

When you own French property the rules concerning its disposition are French. Even if a dispute about ownership or inheritance originates in the UK the law that will decide the outcome will be French.

Livret de famille

Under French law every family is required to keep a *livret de famille* (family booklet). A marriage opens a new *livret* and details of births, adoptions and deaths are added. When a couple divorce two separate copies are created and when a death occurs the *livret* is handed in.

It is an offence not to keep the *livret* up to date. Although the French issue certificates for births, marriages and deaths, it is the livret that provides the onus of proof in the law of inheritance.

Non-French residents are not required to maintain this document. However, the *livret* demonstrates two things:

◆ The French are keen on written evidence. Proving a will in France may prove difficult without a full set of family certificates, affidavits and decrees.

◆ There are important precedents in French civil law about the status of the family and the members of the family group. This begins to explain why rules of succession are more important than the wishes of the individual in matters of inheritance.

Rules of succession

The French are required by law to leave most of their estate to their family. Residents' assets are dealt with under the rules of domicile, but these do not include property, which is always passed on according to French laws of succession.

Precedence is given to ascendant and descendant heirs – the *héritiers reservée. The inheritance rules are:*

◆ One child will inherit at least half the estate.

◆ Two children between them will inherit at least two-thirds of the estate.

◆ Three or more children will share at least three-quarters of the estate. Rules have recently been changed so that, within certain parameters, children do not have to be equally provided for.

◆ The surviving spouse (who is not a héritier reservée) will inherit half, a third, or a quarter of the estate, or a life interest in the estate which will pass to the children on his or her death.

◆ The remaining portion of the estate is freely disposable (*quotite disponible*). If there are no surviving ascendants, descendants, or spouse, the whole estate becomes freely disposable.

◆ The surviving spouse is entitled to continue to enjoy the marital property during his or her lifetime.

Residents have made various attempts to get round the rules of succession. One of these is to set up trusts, but they have generally not been recognised in French courts.

There is one legal way to offset some of the impact of the inheritance rules. This is to arrange the property purchase as a co-ownership with a contract clause that allows the surviving partner to inherit.

The survivor could then choose:

◆ To sell the property and take the net proceeds beyond the rule of French law.

◆ To stay in the property as sole owner. If this happens the estate of the survivor will become subject to the normal rules of domicile and succession.

A French lawyer can draw up a contract of co-ownership, although he would be surprised if he was asked to perform this service for a married couple. Married couples normally arrange for an *en tontine* clause to be incorporated within the deeds at the time of purchase. *En tontine* was originally intended to avoid the break up of large (generally agricultural) estates. Traditionally it meant that those who would ordinarily have rights under the rules of succession are by-passed in favour of the surviving owner, or the last surviving héritier reservée. A similar arrangement was outlawed in the UK more than a century ago because it led, quite literally, to murder.

En tontine in France is now invariably restricted to married couples. When the first partner dies the survivor becomes the absolute owner of the property. Typically the form is:

'. . . *that it is expressly agreed between the purchasers that the first to die will be deemed never to have had any right to the property . . . and the said property will be deemed to always have been that of the survivor.*

'*Until the death of the first purchaser each purchaser shall be a joint owner. Neither of them can sell the property purchased, and any act of management or of disposal must take place with the unanimous consent of the purchasers. The purchasers declare that they have taken into account the chancy nature of this arrangement in determining the share of purchase price payable by each of them.'*

An *en tontine* clause is probably right for married couples if neither partner has children by previous marriages. This is because *en tontine* can be challenged by children on the grounds that the clause deprives them of their rights under France's succession rules.

Under the *en tontine* clause the second (surviving) partner has to pay French succession tax at the rate of 60% of one half of the value of the property. But although neither *en tontine* nor co-ownership avoid succession duties they generally delay their imposition and may also help to ensure that the property is disposed of according to the owner's wishes.

The will as a document

Three kinds of will are provable under French law:

◆ The *testament olographe* is handwritten, signed and dated by the testator. Any written addition, including the signature of a witness invalidates it.

◆ The *testament authentique* is dictated by the testator and witnessed by two *notaires*, or one *notaire* and two adult witnesses.

◆ The *testament mystique* is a handwritten or typescript document signed by the testator and sealed in an envelope in the presence of two witnesses. The witnesses then hand the envelope to a *notaire* who signs the sealed envelope himself. He dates it, notes the names of the witnesses and adds a written declaration that he understands the envelope to contain the will of a named testator.

Rules for validating wills in France are very strict. The more complex the document and the greater the number of witnesses, the more likely it is to become void.

The rules for proving a will in the UK are as different as the kind of document that is acceptable. Rules on intestacy are also different. In France the whole of the property would be divided according to the laws of succession, which favour children. In the UK the law favours the surviving spouse. It is always worth noting that in France marriage does not automatically revoke an existing will.

Intestacy profits nobody but the lawyers, and this is doubly true for double intestacy. The importance of taking good advice when property and assets are held in more than one country cannot be over stressed.

Executors

Under UK law an executor is technically the owner of the testator's assets and property. He discharges the responsibility of ownership by paying debts and duties and distributing the residue estate in accordance with the testator's wishes, as indicated in the will.

In France the position is different. Property is deemed to pass directly to heirs under the rules of succession and an executor is not necessary. Debts and duties are the responsibility of the heirs, but an *executeur testamentaire* may be appointed to help supervise other aspects of the process of inheritance.

This service is important if specific items of furniture and jewellery are intended to pass to named beneficiaries within that part of the estate which is freely disposable (*quotite disponible*). A *notaire* can be appointed to carry out this service but any adult can be asked by the testator to accept the responsibility. The *executeur testamentaire* must be named in the will and should not be one of the major beneficiaries.

MARRIAGE CONTRACTS

The French have a choice as to how assets are held by a married couple. The choice made is recorded as a contract which is drawn up by a *notaire* before the wedding. If no such contract is agreed the law assumes the married couple are subject to the *régime de communaute reduite aux acquets*. Briefly this means that assets belonging to each of the married couple at the time of the marriage remain their personal property but assets later acquired together would be equally divided in the event of divorce. This is by far the most common form of written or implied contract. The alternatives are:

◆ *Régime de la séperation des biens.* This is broadly similar to the legal position in the UK. In effect husband and wife each retain their own assets.

◆ *Régime de la participation aux acquets.* Here the husband places limitations on the sharing of assets.

◆ *Régime de la communaute universelle.* All assets are shared regardless of who brought them to the marriage.

MORTGAGES AND LOANS
When considering mortgage options the UK borrower begins with two basic choices:

Borrowing in the UK against a UK security – normally a new or second mortgage on a property.
Borrowing in France against the security of the property purchased.

It is generally accepted that if you have to borrow it should either be in the currency of your income or in the currency of the country where you are buying the property.

Raising finance in the UK
Banks and building societies compete fiercely for mortgage business but the situation could change rapidly if credit controls are introduced, or if money supply is limited in some other way. If this happens mortgage applications for second homes in particular are unlikely to be regarded with much favour.

It should also be noted:

◆ A mortgage can be secured against assets other than property.

◆ A bank or building society that holds a first mortgage on a UK property may be willing to extend the mortgage facility with a minimum of formalities if the account has been properly conducted.

◆ Banks are usually prepared to lend up to 80% of the total equity value when an additional amount is requested to invest in foreign property.

◆ Any new mortgage or loan is likely to be subject to legal and arrangement fees.

◆ Raising money in the UK may be easier in terms of communication.

◆ When finance is raised in advance in the UK and deposited in a French bank, this is effectively a cash transaction. This can be advantageous in negotiating a reduction in the asking price.

Foreign currency loan

It may also be possible to raise a foreign currency loan secured against UK property. One advantage of this is that the loan can be fixed for a repayment period much shorter than a mortgage. Another advantage is that capital is repaid alongside interest even at the early stages of repayment, something which happens to a much smaller degree with mortgages.

A loan is charged at a higher interest rate than a mortgage, but because the repayment period is shorter, it is likely to prove to be a less expensive option. A loan may be of particular benefit to people approaching retirement age.

One problem with a foreign currency loan is what can happen if the borrower is unable to maintain repayments. If the bank sells the secured property there may be a surplus in sterling terms which becomes a shortfall when converted into foreign currency.

When negotiating loans banks may ask for insurance cover against default in repayments. This cover is to protect the lending institution, not the borrower, and in the event of a claim is paid directly to them.

Endowment mortgage

Borrowers may still be offered loans which include endowments and pension plans. Tied packages of this kind may be more in the interest of the lender than the borrower, who frequently benefits most from a simple repayment scheme. In recent years some forms of endowments have simply not paid off and borrowers should be extremely cautious about entering into this kind of arrangement.

Before signing any loan or mortgage agreement potential borrowers are urged to seek independent financial advice.

Raising finance in France

Many financial institutions in France offer loans, but it is mainly the banks that provide long-term (mortgage) finance.

Some important features of a French loan

♦ Interest rates in France are historically lower than those in the UK and attractive Government subsidies can apply to the purchase of a main residence. These loans are difficult, but not impossible, to obtain. However, if you accept a subsidy loan, you undertake to live in the premises for eight months a year. This in turn means you become legally domiciled in France.

♦ Interest rates are generally fixed for the whole term of the mortgage.

♦ Reversible rate mortgages are negotiable. This means that the interest rate is fixed for a period and then revised within certain boundaries. When interest rates are high this can be a good option.

♦ French financial institutions charge around 1% of the loan as an arrangement fee.

♦ Some borrowers may be eligible for a special savings (épargne logement) loan. These are below normal rates and do not require the purchaser to become domiciled in France.

♦ Loans can be negotiated in a number of different currencies. The US dollar, Swiss franc and German mark, and more recently, the euro, have all been seen at one time or another as advantageous to the borrower. This is partly speculative, and partly created by a market perception that some currencies are more stable than others.

◆ Security on the property will be required for all loans, which will never be for more than 80% of the purchase price. Premiums for life, health and disablement insurance are included in monthly repayments.

◆ You will not be sold endowment or pension mortgage packages by French banks. These do not exist in France.

◆ The law provides a 'cooling off' period (minimum ten days) after a formal loan offer has been received.

When checking current repayment rates of UK and French mortgages it is important to compare like with like. Take into account the term of years offered (normally shorter in France) and add in insurances, arrangement and legal fees. UK financial institutions are coy about revealing the rates of commission they earn for setting up certain types of loans and mortgages, but sometimes these can add hundreds of euros a year to your payments.

The following major French insitutions are enthusiastic enough about UK mortgage business to have opened offices on this side of the Channel. They also provide brochures and free information:

Banque Transatlanique
36 St James St
London SW1A 1JD
☎ 020 7493 6717

Crédit Agricole
11 Moorfields Highwalk
London EC2Y 9DE
☎ 020 7374 5000

Crédit Lyonnais
Suite 57
1 Colme St
Edinburgh EH3 6AA
☎ 0131 220 8257

Crédit du Nord
6th Floor, Exchange House
Primrose St
London EC2A 2ED
☎ 020 7488 0872

In addition to the major banking organisations loans can be negotiated through savings banks (caisses d'épargne) and *notaires*. All loans are subject to your financial status and the general rule that your mortgage repayments should not add up to more than 30% of your gross income.

INSURANCE

Insurance requirements in France are different to the UK:

◆ The law demands that every property is covered by third-party insurance (*civil propriété*). *If your property is to be built the premium must be paid before work on the site begins.*

- French morgage lenders (unlike their UK equivalents) do not insist that you take out buildings insurance. However, it is strongly recommended that you do. This can be arranged separately or included in a comprehensive (*multirisque*) policy that also covers your possessions. UK insurers generally offer the most complete and competitive policies.

- If you live in a block of flats the *civil propriété* and the buildings policies will be paid communally. Check your lease or the terms of the sale agreement. In communal (co-owned) property you always have adequate cover for your possessions.

- If you let out your property, or allow someone to live in it, the tenant should indemnify you against the risk of fire. He is also responsible for insuring his own possessions.

6

The purchase process

More than 50% of properties are bought through estate agencies.

THE FRENCH ESTATE AGENT

The *agent immobilier* is rather more respected in France than the UK. This may be partly because the profession is highly regulated. Before he can set up in business, he must have:

◆ Standards of qualification, competence and experience.

◆ A professional permit to cover all property transactions. The permit has to be revalidated annually by the local *préfecture de police*.

◆ Professional indemnity insurance.

◆ Bank guarantees that cover him for all money he holds on behalf of clients. It is illegal for him to hold any money if the guarantee is for less than €85,000.

◆ Up to date knowledge of the true cost of transactions and market values. He is required by law to give this information and to give it honestly.

◆ Power of attorney (*mandat de vente*) before he can negotiate any sale on behalf of the vendor. The *mandat* has to be renewed after three months. He cannot purchase any property himself for which he holds a *mandat* for sale.

◆ Specified rates of commission written into the power of attorney and prominently displayed in his office.

Payments to agents

Traditionally, in France the purchaser, rather than the vendor, who has to pay the agent's commission.

But this is no longer universally so. Agents in some regions have now adopted the more common EU practice of charging the vendor.

It makes little difference in the end. The commission is usually hidden in the purchase price if the vendor pays it, or a property may seem unusually cheap if commission is to be added. Commission rates were fixed by law until 1987 but agents now charge whatever they think the market can stand. In practice they usually ask 5% (plus TVA at 18.6%) but the rate can be higher for up-market properties. Sometimes a sliding scale is used. In either event the agent must display his scale of charges.

No commission is payable until the sale is legally finalised by the writing and recording of the deed.

THE UK ESTATE AGENT

An increasingly large number of UK estate agents are represented in France. Most commonly these are 'piggyback' operations where the UK agency is adjoined to a French agency. Some agencies, however, have associations with French agents as well as their own regional offices.

But a few agencies do things differently. They attract custom at UK-based exhibitions and 'profile' new customers before promising to find French property that suits the buyer's budget and personal preferences. They claim to provide a one-stop service intended to deal with every aspect of the purchase process.

But the process is not always as straightforward and transparent as the publicity suggests. Included in one 'package', for instance, is advice on *'rights of way'*, *'land divisions'*, 'making a will', etc. The same agency even talk about *'popping in for a cup of tea to see how you are getting along after the purchase'*. They also encourage the view that a successful gîte or bed and breakfast business can be up and running within a few weeks and that continued support and assistance will be available to help make this possible.

Prospective purchasers should be careful about these claims. On occasion, buyers have been brusquely informed, following the purchase, that continued agency expertise, or a referral to an appropriate professional, is indeed available –

at €100 an hour. And, although their fee is 'all inclusive' (including legal work and taxes) 'one-stop services' do not come cheaply. One agent's scale of charges in 2002 ran from a minimum of €550. For the purchase of a €30,000 property in the Charente, in the same year, the agent's bill was €880. In effect, the purchaser paid twice the normal cost of the transaction process.

The buyer must decide for himself whether this kind of 'bells and frills' package is worth the premium rates charged. Judging by the dissatisfaction of some customers it is certainly worth checking the small print. Communication throughout an English solicitor may be an advantage, but this assumes that French estate agents and lawyers are poor communicators. They are not.

It is also worth noting that matters such as '*rights of way*' and '*land divisions*', etc. are routinely checked by the lawyer handling the legal work, and that some other elements of the package – such as '*drawing up a will*' – can be done separately and relatively inexpensively. It is also worth asking if it is realistic to turn a property – which could require some renovation – into a successful business within a few weeks.

And, if communication remains an issue, there is an excellent network of UK agents offering the same services at the same scale of charges as their French colleagues. www.real-estate-european-union.com has definitive listings. You will also find valuable advice delivered with the voice of integrity and experience at www.findaproperty.co.uk and www.hamptons-int.com

THE NOTAIRE

The French solitior, the *notaire*, is a highly qualified and respected individual:

◆ His authority is necessary to create valid contracts.

◆ His occupation is strictly regulated by the Ministry of Justice and his professional association the *Chambre de Notaires*.

◆ He is entitled to act (and usually does) for both parties in a property sale.

◆ He is obliged to explain impartially the implications of the clauses of contract.

◆ He is entitled to act as sales negotiator – taking on the role of the *agent immobilier* – for which he receives a commission.

◆ He is invariably employed to negotiate complex sales such as those that involve co-ownership, or after death or divorce.

◆ He draws up the authentic act of sale, verifies the vendor's right to sell, checks planning regulations and notes existing charges against the property. Where these are greater than the sale price he must be sure that the creditors can be paid in some other way.

◆ He is responsible for collecting registration fees and passing them on to the appropriate authorities.

Preliminary contracts

A contract for the sale of property in France is more like

the Scottish system than the English. Once a preliminary contract has been signed it is difficult and expensive to back out of the deal. One advantage of the system is that gazumping is almost unknown in France.

There are two forms of contract in current use:

Compromis de vente

Signing the *compromis de vente* – literally compromise or implication of sale – means that vendor and purchaser are committed. It is possible to include 'get out' clauses in the contract (*conditions suspensives*) but these will relate to obtaining a mortgage, checking the authority to sell and town planning reports.

Conditions suspensives take precedence over other contract clauses. If they cannot be fulfilled the contract becomes void and deposits are returned.

The compromis de vente is the normal form of agreement in a private sale. The contract can include agreed penalty clauses to be imposed on either vendor or purchaser if the sale breaks down for any reason other than those listed in the conditions. All such conditions are clearly set out in the document. These include:

◆ The responsibilities of the vendor and purchaser.

◆ Any easements that affect the property – such as public footpaths.

◆ Any government pre-emptive rights – such as water testing or special regional development projects.

♦ The *conditions suspensives.*

♦ The agreed price and method of payment.

A deposit is paid – normally 10% – on the signing of the *compromis de vente.* This is held by a third party (the *agent immobilier* or the *notaire*) until final contracts are signed.

Properties are usually bought as seen in France because owners are bound by law to reveal all the defects they are aware of. Unfortunately this is no guarantee that all is well. In the event of a problem arising after sale the purchaser finds himself in the unenviable position of having to prove that the fault was likely to be known before the signing of the *compromis de vente.* For properties more than ten years old the services of a surveyor (*expert geometre*) are recommended. A full structural survey is expensive, but much cheaper than dealing with an infestation of woodworm.

The promesse de vente

This is a shortened version of the *compromis de vente.* Here a time for completion is set against an agreed price and certain legal conditions and requirements.

Although the buyer has a period of 'time to reflect' he is still likely to lose his deposit if he pulls out of the deal.

The *Promesse* is really a unilateral agreement to sell, whereas the *compromis* is binding on both parties. As the purchaser is the most likely party to go back on the agreement the *promesse* has few advantages for him. The bilateral *compromis* is the contract to go for.

Whichever agreement is signed, this leads to the *acte authentique* which is the final conveyance of the property from seller to buyer.

The acte authentique

The *notaire* will produce a draft contract (*projet de l'acte*) a week or so before the completion date. This is sent out with a letter of convocation which reminds both parties of the date agreed to meet and sign the final agreement.

A sample bill

Agreed price of property – €100,000

Sliding scale fees:

For first €3333 (at 5%)	€166
For next €3333 (at 3.3%)	€110
For next €11666 (at 1.65%)	€191
For next €81,666 (0.85%)	€693
VAT on the above (at 18.6%)	€216

Registration fees:

Départmentale (at 4.2%)	€4,200
Communale (at 1.2%)	€1,200
Régionale (at 1.2%)	€1,200
Hypothèques (at 0.1%)	€100

Stamp duty (at 0.6%)	€600

Total (8.7% of property price)	€8,676

The *acte authentique* is essentially the same contract as the *compromis de vente*. Additionally it will:

◆ Clearly identify the property and land.

◆ Provide an analysis of ownership rights for at least the previous 30 years. Where the property itself is new this will only refer to ownership of the land.

◆ Refer to searches made and certificates issued. These relate to planning regulations, easements and guarantees.

Power of attorney

French law requires both parties to be present at the signing of contracts. This could involve an English purchaser in extra journeys to France, unless he signs a *mandat* (power of attorney). This can be given to the *agent immobilier* or the *notaire* and permits him to sign the contracts on your behalf.

ADDITIONAL COST OF PURCHASE

There is no such thing as a typical transaction because the *agent immobilier* may charge either vendor or purchaser. Notaries, however, charge on a scale of fees that relate to the agreed sale price. The following list is fairly typical:

First €3,333 of purchase price – 5%
From €3,334 to €6,666 – 3.3%
From €6,667 to €18,333 – 1.65%
Rest of purchase price – 0.85%

There are five additional fees payable when purchasing a property. These are again percentages of property price:

◆ *tax départmentale* – 4.2%

◆ tax communale – 1.2%

◆ *tax regionale* which varies but is typically about 1.2%

◆ stamp duty – 0.6%

◆ land transfer register (conservateur des hypothèques) 0.1%

Most of these fees are similar to those payable for searches, notices and authentications in the UK.

If 5% (€5000) is added for *agent immobilier* fees the total becomes €13,676 – or 13.68% of the property price.

If the *notaire* also negotiates the sale (acts as *agent immobilier*) he almost invariably charges different rates for this service. Typically they would be:

For first €29,166 (at 5%) €1,458
For next €70,833 (2.5%) €1,770
Promesse de vente (at 0.3%) €300
VAT on the above (at 18.6%) €656

Total €4,184

The alternative grand total becomes €12,865 – or 12.87% of the property price. It is invariably cheaper to buy through a *notaire*.

COMPANY PROPERTY PURCHASE

It is possible to set up a company for the purpose of buying French property. The most commonly acknowledged advantage of this is that the company shares are not subject to French inheritance tax. There are, however, possible dis-advantages with regards to capital gains and company taxes and the need to claim certain tax exemptions before annual deadlines. The company may also need to appoint a fiscal agent and will certainly require the services of a French accountant. A company property purchase is therefore only worth considering if the property purchase(s) are on a fairly large scale.

$$\boxed{7}$$

Building or buying a property under construction

In the UK it is generally accepted that building a house – or having it built for you – is the cheapest way of buying a property. The same is almost certainly true in France.

BUILDING LAND

The French divide land into zones – *residentiel, artisanal* and *industriel*. If land is defined on town plans as *residentiel* then domestic building is permitted as long as bylaws and regulations are followed.

Planning permission

Planning permission (*permis de construire*) is not, as it is in England, permission to build. The right to build is implied when you buy building land – a *terrain a batir*. However, permission is required to erect a specific building on a specific site. If your property is a 'model' (pre-determined type) from a reputable builder, then planning permission is likely to be a formality and will only take two weeks to obtain.

THE COST OF BUILDING

Most building is done through a development company. These companies invariably provide a number of 'model' properties at attractive prices. The 'models' have been designed to meet with local planning regulations. Internal modifications can be negotiated subject to building regulations.

Many of these agencies have high street offices and can be mistaken for estate agents. The prices of the 'packages' are often prominently displayed.

Base prices

The base price for typical models is about:

2 bedroom bungalow with garage, approx. 80 m^2 – €47,000
3 bedroom bungalow with garage, approx. 120 m^2 – €58,000
4 bedroom family house and garage, approx. 180 m^2 – €97,000

Land prices

The cost of building land – the *terrain de batir* – must be added to the base price. City and suburban land can be expensive, as can building plots with sea frontage. Elsewhere building land usually costs between €30 and €35 per square metre. Land has barely risen at all in price over the past 20 years. In 2003 it was still possible to buy land with outline planning permission for as little as €19 per square metre.

Designated building plots are usually about 500 square metres in the larger towns and cities, between 500 and 1000 square metres in coastal areas, and about 50% bigger inland.

A 700–800 square metre building plot may cost around €24,000 on the coast. The same money would buy a larger plot inland.

A 700 square metre plot could be 35 metres long by 20 metres wide. A two-bedroomed bungalow, with garage, or a three-bedroomed bungalow without garage, or a four-bedroomed house with garage might have a floor area of 12 metres by 8 metres. This would leave you with a garden area about the size of a tennis court.

Supplementary costs

The following checklist provides estimates of supplementary costs:

Connections for electricity and water	€2,000
Local taxes and consents	€2,950
Notaires fees for land purchase	€1,170

Total costs

A breakdown of costs for the construction of a three bed-room bungalow (120 square metres including garage) built on a plot of land of about 750 square metres would break down like this:

Construction of property	€56,000
Purchase of land	€24,000
Connection of utilities	€2,000
Local taxes and consents	€2,950
Notaires fees	€1,170
Total	€86,120

For comparison purposes the national index target price for new (rural) properties of this specification is €121,080. The implication is that having a house built saves about one-quarter of the asking price of a finished property. It is a powerful incentive.

Building 'packages' in France are fairly complete and include allowances for fitted kitchens, bathroom suites and decoration. Gardens are usually 'landscaped' as part of the deal, but this can mean little more than levelling and removing rubble.

Find out exactly what you can expect for your money by asking to see completed examples of the builder's work. If he will not oblige look for another builder.

THE BUILDING CONTRACT

The nature of the contract is defined by French law. It will include:

♦ A definition of what is to be built.

♦ The quality standards required by the Civil Code.

♦ The schedule of construction and other work.

♦ Penalty clauses for late completion by the builder or late payment by the purchaser.

♦ Information about the land including assumed access rights.

♦ Insurance required during the construction period.

♦ The schedule of stage payments.

Building contracts are not standardised in the same way as those for lettings and normal house purchases.

The time between signing a contract and occupying the property is normally four to six months.

Stage payments

Standards in the construction industry are controlled and are normally high. The French do not have an equivalent expression to 'cowboy builders', which is reassuring, but some construction companies have better reputations than others. Good local research can pay dividends.

Stage payments offer some protection to the customer if the builder goes bust, but if a second company is employed to complete work it will inevitably be more expensive.

The normal pattern of stage payments is:

3% after planning permission and signing the contract
10% on completion of the foundations
20% on completion of the building shell
20% when water connections are complete
15% when electricity connections are complete
15% when heating and plumbing is operational
10% after landscaping work is complete
5% on completion of interior decoration
2% on the handing over of keys

Do not part with any money until the building permit has been granted. Most developers seek permission to develop a number of plots on land they own so a permit is not usually a problem, but it is the only guarantee you have that the building is legal. If it is not, the administrative bodies can demand that you return the land to its original condition. The risk is the same if the building does not comply with the authorisation, so make sure that the house you are having built is the same as the one in the permit. Modifications require a second building permit.

French financial institutions are familiar with stage payments and loans can be phased in accordingly.

DOING IT YOURSELF

It is theoretically possible to build your own house in France, but the sight of UK vehicles with roof racks laden with building materials is not particularly common.

First steps

Assuming the land you wish to buy is designated as building land on the town plan, you also need to ensure:

◆ Suitable access is provided.

◆ Local bylaws are compiled with.

◆ A building permit is required for a building that has a floor surface (*la surface hors d'oeuvre*) of more than 20 square metres and for any external modification that changes the appearance of an existing building.

◆ The building must meet *coefficient d'occupation des sols* (*COS*) guidelines. This is a formula that relates building to the total constructible ground surface. In densely populated areas the coefficient may be one: this means you build on all the land available. Elsewhere the coefficient can vary between 50 and 10%. At 50% you need 200 square metres of land to build a 100 square metre building, at 10% you will need 1,000 square metres of land.

Advice is available from local *mairies*.

Supplementary costs

When land is purchased the services of a *notaire* are required. If a loan is needed either for the land acquisition, or for the property construction, fees will be charged for financial advice, for administration and for registering the loan.

A survey (*geometre*) is also required. Fees for this purpose are likely to be between €500 and €850.

The *compromis de vente* will obtain a clause that makes the new landowner fence off his boundaries. The cost of this has recently been estimated at €20 per running metre. A typical plot of about 700 metres would therefore cost around €2,200 to fence.

Getting the permit

La surface hors d'oeuvre is defined as the total ground area of a building. For buildings of more than one storey the total of all the stories are added together, including attics and basements. *La surface* also includes the thickness of external walls, balconies and terraces. The services of an architect (or a building company that employs an architect) are required for any building over 170 square metres.

While many properties are below 170 square metres in size this should not be seen as a licence to manage without professional back-up. Only someone with specialised knowledge will be able to draw up the required documentation for planning approval. This includes:

◆ A detailed site plan that includes trees, existing outbuildings, boundaries and access.

◆ A scale drawing of the proposed building that includes all the elevations.

◆ A rather complex form (PC 157) must be completed and returned to the local *mairie*. Notification is given of the hearing at which all aspects of the proposed construction will be discussed. The application can be rejected on either architectural or environmental grounds.

If the proposed building is near an historical site or monument the application is automatically referred to the *Architect des Batiments de France*. He will visit the site before making a ruling.

Planning permission refused

If your plans are refused you have two options:

◆ To submit modified plans, or to accept any suggested modifications.

◆ To appeal to the local administrative court (*le Tribunal Administratif*).

This can be a long process and is not recommended.

The secret of success is to talk informally to officials at the local *mairie* as you are preparing your plans. They know what is likely to be acceptable and what will be rejected out of hand.

Plans for improvements

The 20 square metre rule applies, and formal applications

are required for projects larger than this. Any changes to an existing property must also come within the COS guidelines.

A declaration of intent is signed (form PC156) and sent to the *mairie* by registered post. This must be accompanied by:

◆ A site plan.

◆ Listings of specification and materials.

◆ Plans of existing structures that will be modified, or photographs with the modifications drawn in.

If there is no reply within one calendar month you can assume the application is approved.

BUYING A PROPERTY UNDER CONSTRUCTION

Despite the popular impression that UK buyers are all looking for cottages in Provence or the Dordogne, most opt to buy flats or new houses on the Channel and Atlantic coasts.

Buying on plan

Buying '*en etat futur d'achievement*' is a well known purchase arrangement in France. Stage payments are similar to those for building through a developer and the law is again on the side of the buyer. It lays down the maximum percentage payment allowed for each stage of completion, and money does not become due until architects and surveyors have issued the necessary approvals. The buyer is also protected against minor defects for two years, and against major ones for ten.

There are few bargains to be had 'buying on plan' because developments are nearly always on prime sites (often close to the sea) and they are invariably finished to high standards. Some 90% of such developments are apartment buildings.

In some cases the purchaser will literally see nothing more than plans and drawings. Developments are usually phased, and a second phase is an indication that the first has been successful. You should be suspicious of a development that has been completed but a number of apartments remain unsold.

The main points of the contract are:

◆ The particular apartment is identified and described, and the price is fixed.

◆ The development schedule is explained.

◆ All stage payments and conditions of sale are set out.

Advantages of buying 'on plan'
'On plan' purchases are popular because:

◆ Buyers are getting a new property.

◆ Although 'on plan' apartments are at the pricier end of the market, the value of the finished apartment is invariably greater than the *prix fermé*. Stage payments allow the developer to maintain his cash flow throughout the development process, rather than having to wait to sell the finished article. The purchaser in turn is rewarded for his 'act of faith' by having the price fixed for up to two years ahead of completion.

◆ If apartments are sold direct, the *prix fermé* can represent a 5% discount as no estate agent is involved.

◆ The purchaser can inspect the property at various stages of development. He can choose his own scheme of decoration, colour of bathroom suite, kitchen units and applicances, and can select floor tiles from a pre-determined range.

◆ Some buyers take the advantage of stage payments by delaying loan applications, or by taking their time to dispose of other assets. Some hold cash reserves on deposit and arrange withdrawals in line with the payment schedule.

◆ Contracts rarely have severe penalty clauses for late payments. A month's 'grace' is common, followed by a penalty charge of around 1% per month.

◆ Contracts of co-ownership usually take six to eight weeks to complete and *notaires* can spin things out longer than that. This means the buyer has to find only the deposit (usually 5%), followed by the stage payments due by the date of completion.

◆ Banks are often less cautious about lending money 'on plan' than for other property purchases. This is because equity values are easy to determine, the developers are often large, successful (and solvent) companies, and the apartments themselves are easy to dispose of if repossession becomes necessary.

◆ Developers can often arrange attractive mortgage terms. The developer, of course, earns commission and the bank increases its volume of mortgage business.

◆ Legal costs may be reduced if one *notaire* is used by the developer and a number of co-owners. This is because research time and paperwork is reduced, and contracts can be drafted 'in blocks'.

◆ Power of attorney (*mandat*) is often designated to third parties who will attend the *acte de vente* on behalf of the buyer. This power of attorney is not a short-cut but a safeguard. A professional – familiar with the French language and civil law – is more likely to make sense of the procedure and to identify any last-minute problems. This can also save the purchaser time and money by making an additional journey from the UK necessary.

Spotting the sharks

Although 'on plan' purchases are generally satisfactory some buyers have been disappointed, or worse still, ripped off.

It is not unknown for 'phantom developers' to set up a mobile office (generally during the holiday season) and to take deposits for a project they have little or no intention of completing. At best this is testing the market, and at worst it is fraud. Either way it will be difficult to get your money back.

Bona fide developers go to great lengths to market their apartments. They produce well drafted plans, glossy literature and can generally point to a track record of success. If you are in any doubt ask around locally or check at the *mairie*.

When a development is not selling well the developer may sell a few apartments to a third party at a greatly reduced price. This third party (often an estate agent) will then offer the apartments at slightly below the *prix ferme*. The purchaser buys from the agent, who adds his fees into the sale price. Later he finds himself paying the developer – not the agent – the outstanding stage payments.

This is legal and it can prove to be a bargain. In most cases, however, it suggests that the developer was over optimistic in forecasting profit margins. The resale value of the apartments may reflect this.

When an agent is selling several apartments in the same development be suspicious. It may be that he has been appointed to sell all the apartments – which happens – but it could also be an opportunist attempt to unload undesirable property.

Your property as a *gîte* business

Many buyers of French property intend to let them out at certain times of the year. This can be an informal arrangement – letting to friends and family perhaps – or it can be a full blown *gîte* business.

As a first principle it is important not to blur the distinction between a *gîte* business and a guest house. If you offer services such as reception, daily cleaning, bedding and linen and baby-sitting these may be classified as para-hotel services which could mean you must register for TVA (VAT). This in turn means you will then have to charge your guests the reduced rate (5.5%) for the accommodation and the full rate (20.6%) for the other services. In practice this is applied by charging the lower rate on 75% of the receipts and the higher rate on the remaining 25%. In addition to this you will have to pay the so-called professional duty – a tax so complicated that it requires a professional to unravel it.

The lesson is to try to limit what you offer to little more than the accommodation. This does not mean you will completely escape the long arm of the taxman. Those who do not register for TVA have to pay lease duty – 2.5% of your receipts – unless the total receipts do not exceed €1,800 a year. You will also have to pay land tax. You will, however, avoid habitation tax on the part of the building that is available exclusively for renting.

The right place

If you intend to have a successful business certain locations are much better than others.

The most popular tourist areas are largely seasonal. This means that it is all too easy to have unrealistic expectations as to the possible returns. Only the Alps and the Côte d'Azur have anything approaching a year-round season. The season in much of northern and central France is generally no more than 12 to 14 weeks. That said, there are areas, particularly close to the Channel ports, which, with targeted promotion, can produce a year-round return. However, the southern half of Brittany remains firmly the first choice of the UK *gîte* buyer largely because the area offers a unique combination of lower property values, good summer climate, the attractions of the Atlantic coast and reasonable accessibility. The Loire Atlantique and the Dordogne also remain popular with UK buyers, although property bargains are more difficult to find than they were a decade ago.

A practical decision

Buying a *gîte* should be a practical rather than an emotional decision. A property that will convert into several small units has much to recommend it. There are plenty of *gîtes* available for large families or families sharing accommodation. There are relatively few offering good quality accommodation for four people or less. Buying a property as a *gîte* should have more to do with gaps in the market than your own preferences.

Practicality also dictates that you consider the following questions before turning your French property into a *gîte* business:

◆ Have you taken into account the cost of equipping the *gîte* with furniture and fittings?

◆ Will it cost more to convert than you could sell it for after conversion?

◆ Have you taken the security of an empty property into consideration?

◆ Who will manage the property, clean and check it between lettings?

◆ Will having the property as a business affect the terms and conditions of your mortgage and insurance?

GÎTES AND THE LAW

The formalities of buying a *gîte* are the same as those for buying any other residential property. However you should:

◆ **Inform the *notaire* of your intention.** He will add the appropriate clause into the *acte de vente*, which saves additional paperwork later on.

◆ **Inform the *Registre de Commerce* and the tax authorities.** If you fail to do so punitive financial penalties can be applied.

Gites ruraux

All *gîte* are registered in France according to the facilities they offer. Most are fairly basic and are counted as *gîtes ruraux* (rural accommodation). There are tax allowances that can be claimed as long as the property is let out for a minimum of three months each year.

Promoting the property

Promotion is something that is frequently overlooked. A successful *gîte* business is one that attracts business outside the high season and one which customers will return to year after year. To achieve this a full promotional strategy should be planned at least 12 months before the first letting is anticipated.

The options

The most cost effective way is to promote it yourself and to live close enough to the property to manage it. If this is not viable you must consider the alternatives:

◆ You can use an international agency. Commission rates are high – up to 20% but they do pay in a currency and place of your choice. One major problem with these agencies is that they offer no supplementary services.

They only provide property guides and process bookings. Important considerations such as inventories, main- tenance, cleaning, laundry and the general welfare of the property remain your responsibility.

◆ You can appoint a French agent. Commission rates are again high – around 15% but the agent will manage the property on your behalf. Bills, which include repairs and replacements, are usually added to the agent's com- mission. This can prove to be expensive.

◆ You can promote the property yourself and appoint a local manager. Your estate agent, *notaire* or bank may be able to suggest someone suitable. Failing that there are a number of local agencies that specialise in this kind of business. Your nearest *Syndicat d'Initiative* (tourist information office) should be able to make a recom- mendation.

Advertising

Most promotional budgets are around 10% of net income, and rather more than that in the first year. Do not overlook the value of free publicity. Your local *Syndicat d'Initiative* will list the property and respond to enquiries on your behalf. It pays dividends to keep them up to date on availability.

A number of UK publications are worth considering. *The Guardian, The Independent, The Telegraph, The Mail on Sunday* and *The Sunday Times* have all developed a solid reputation among *gîte* owners. *The Yorkshire Post, Evening Standard, Manchester Evening News* and *Birmingham Post* lead the way among regional newspapers. *The Lady* remains the first choice magazine.

When placing the advertisement make sure that you include as a minimum the following information:

◆ The exact location of the *gîte*.

◆ The dates of availability.

◆ The tariff structure. This is most frequently quoted as 'prices from . . .' with high season prices being up to double the stated amount.

◆ The number of beds.

◆ Local facilities for sport and recreation.

◆ A telephone contact number and email address.

MAKING A PROFIT

For a *gîte* owner this is not necessarily a pre-requisite. The purpose is usually to make some return on your investment. An incalculable factor in this is your own enjoyment of the property.

The tariff structure

You are obviously going to charge most in high season, but your rates should be competitive throughout the letting period. The amount you can ask depends on the property itself and its location, so comparing your *gîte* with similar properties is the best way to find out what the market can stand.

You must also be clear about exactly what you are offering. Household linen, insurance and telephone charges are not normally included in self-catering tariffs. Tourist taxes and cleaning usually are. A few years ago guests were expected to pay for metered electricity. This is now usually included in the price, though supplementary charges for heating in winter are not uncommon.

Scanning newspaper columns in late 2003 revealed that high season *gîte* tariffs ranged from €650 a week for basic four bed accommodation to €2,600 for a small chateau with room for 17. Most *gîte* owners were asking between €750 and €1,000 a week.

A formula for success

Every *gîte* business is different but there are common factors to consider in working out the potential profitability:

◆ Income is often worked out over a maximum letting period of 36 weeks which is broken down into three 12-week blocks of high, medium and low tariffs.

◆ Expenditure is calculated over the same time scale. This includes advertising, cleaning and refurbishment for the letting period, plus a portion of the annual bills. These bills include loans, insurances and local taxes.

◆ Deducting expenditure from income gives you a pre-tax profit figure. If this is less than 10% of the market value of the property then the business, from a purely financial point of view, should be regarded as unsuccessful. This was in the days when a similar income could have been generated by investing the amount of the loan in a building society. Five or six percent may now be regarded as a respectable return and you can take comfort though from the fact that there are 16 weeks left to enjoy the *gîte* yourself.

Sample calculation

As a simple rule of thumb, if the property is let for three-quarters of the year, then three-quarters of the annual bills can be set against income.

Value of property €65,000

Income

12 weeks at €650 =	€7,800
12 weeks at €400 =	€4,800
12 weeks at €300 =	€3,600
Total	€16,200

Expenditure

Proportion of annual loan repayments	€3,850
Proportion of utilities and local charges	€1,000
Cleaning and management	€2,000
Advertising	€800
Repairs	€500
Replacements	€150
Total	€8,300

Pre-tax profit	€7,900

Not many *gîte* owners achieve anything like this sort of return. This is because it is often unrealistic to assume it possible to let for 36 weeks a year while overheads will remain fairly constant. But even sustaining a loss need not be a disaster. The property itself is an investment and there are owners who suggest that persuading others to pay part of their mortgage is success in itself. The important thing is to approach the possible outcomes realistically. Certainly there are trouble-free investments that may prove more profitable.

A fringe benefit of a *gîte* business is that the French tax authorities allow you to offset refurbishment costs against letting income. This should mean, in the early years at least, your tax bill should be negligible.

THE GÎTE AS A BUSINESS

A *gîte* business counts as self employment in France. You are not only taxable but you will have to pay social security contributions. You must register yourself with the local chamber of commerce (Chambre de Commerce) which will require:

◆ A *carte de sejour*. (See Chapter 4)

◆ An attestation from your *notaire* that the property is legally yours.

◆ Your passport and additional passport photographs.

◆ Your birth and marriage certificate, and possibly other family documentation.

And a word of warning. The largest association of French estate agents, the FNAIM, works alongside the tax authorities to enforce advertising and tax legislation. One effect of this is a review of internet sites offering holiday lettings. In April 2004 it was revealed that around 350 sites, many of British origin, were under scrutiny.

If the *Chambre de Commerce* is satisfied with your bona fides you will be entered on the register as a *louer en meubles professionnel* – a professional renter of furnished accommodation.

You are now in the *gîte* business.

9

Setting up a business in France

THE PROFESSIONAL ADVISORS

A *gîte* business is an obvious choice for those choosing to maximise the profitability of their French property assets. Compared with the bureaucratic nightmare of setting up any other kind of business the *gîte* is also wrapped in less red tape.

But apart from a *gîte* business it is very possibly commercial insanity to consider running any kind of trading activity in which you do not already have experience. The penalties for making even honest mistakes are draconian. For instance, for beginning work before registration formalities are complete you could be fined up to €16,000, have your equipment confiscated, be deported or imprisoned, and be banned from carrying on any trading activity in France for three years. It is therefore essential to obtain legal advice before making any transactions that could be construed as trading.

An early point of contact will be the *notaire*. Even if you intend to work from home you are required to set up the business formally and to follow registration procedures. Local town halls also provide valuable advice.

You should also contact:

French Chamber of Commerce
21 Dartmouth Street
Westminster
London
SW1H 9HP
☎ 020 7304 4040

British Business Centre
BP21
14700 Falaise
☎ 03 31 40 05 77

The notaire

The *notaire* again acts on behalf of all parties to a contract for the purchase of a business and commercial property. The final stage of contract – the *acte de vente* is again a notarised deed which only the *notaire* can complete.

His fees for the purchase of an existing small business – a *fonds de commerce* are normally between 16 and 18% of the purchase price.

The agent immobilier

Most business sales are handled in the early stages by an *agent immobilier*. He draws up preliminary contracts and can complete all formalities except for the *acte de vente*.

This is invariably a cheaper option. Total commission charges are likely to be between eight and ten percent of the agreed purchase price.

The advocat or conseil jurisdique

The closest equivalent to these professionals in the UK is perhaps the specialist legal executive. Their offices are most commonly found in Paris and the larger cities.

Since 1991 the role of the *avocat* and *conseil* have been formally identical. Like the *agent immobilier* they can complete all formalities except for authenticating the final contract.

For the purchase of a business there are distinct advantages in using the services of an *avocat.*

- ◆ They are invariably specialists at setting up different kinds of companies and often work exclusively in the commercial area.

- ◆ They can offer advice on commercial and fiscal matters.

- ◆ They will have an up to date understanding of civil and employment legislation.

- ◆ They charge at an agreed hourly rate, which is invariably cheaper than the commission rates of agents and *notaires.*

WHAT KIND OF COMPANY?

French law allows a bewildering range of different kinds of companies. Each has a separate identity.

The most common are:

Société à responsabilité limitée

Very similar to the UK limited company. Liability is limited to at least two, and no more than 50 shareholders, who are expected to have an annual general meeting. The minimum legal share capital is €8,000. Although it may seem rather technical this is probably the best option for the husband and wife team who intend to work mainly from home.

Enterprise unipersonnelle à responsibilité limitée

This is an alternative version of the limited company. It permits a single shareholder with €8,000 share capital. This form of limited liability is a sensible option for the small trader or individual who is working from home.

Enterprise individuelle

Similar to the UK sole trader. This is an inexpensive option to set up but liability is unlimited. It is really only suitable for a part-time or small turnover business, but it remains the most common option for those who choose to work from home.

Société civile

This style of company requires at least two named shareholders. No shareholding capital is involved but liability is apportioned according to the number of shares held. This format is most common when a business is based on land ownership.

Société en commandite

An unusual hybrid company set up. It involves active and sleeping partners. Active partners are fully liable, but the liability of sleeping partners is limited to the amount they have put into the business.

Société en non collectif

Here there are no minimum capital restrictions for at least two shareholders. These shareholders are responsible for company debts, but are treated as sole traders for tax and social security payments.

Société anonyme

This is a common format for companies that hope to attract venture capital in return for possibly a high turnover and large profits. There are at least seven shareholders with a minimum total shareholding of €35,000. Shares may be bought on a subscription basis over a period of five years.

Succersale

This amounts to a branch office. Formalities are limited to registering the company and its articles of incorporation. The French branch office keeps independent accounts. Trading practices, tax and social security matters become subject to French law.

The definition of what constitutes a French branch office or agency – the *succersale* – is a complex one. Essentially the

French authorities will look at the way business is conducted. Key pointers include:

◆ Whether or not contracts, invoices and receipts are issued locally.

◆ Is at least one member of the branch staff resident in France for most of the year?

◆ Is a local manager conducting business negotiations directly with customers?

The advantages of the branch office include:

◆ The cheapness and lack of formality required to establish it.

◆ The branch office's profits and losses can be taken into account in accounting the parent company's income.

Subsidaire

This is an alternative to the branch office. The subsidiary is characterised by the decision making and economic control of the parent company. It is nevertheless fully registered as a French company and subject to French law and taxation.

The subsidiary is more complex and expensive to establish than the branch office. However, it offers certain advantages:

◆ Greater management flexibility because of an autonomous legal stature.

◆ Parent company liability is limited to a modest stake in the subsidiary's capital.

◆ The subsidiary can pay the parent company for finanicial and tehcnical services. These costs can be deducted from taxable income.

◆ The subsidiary allows the parent company to cooperate with third parties in France which acquire holdings.

Bureau de liason

This is sometimes called a shop window. It is the legal form that allows a foreign business to communicate with potential customers – normally through advertising.

This requires the minimum of formalities, and is not normally subject to French corporation tax. In order to comply with EU regulations the bureau must not have any commercial, industrial or service activity. Officially activities are limited to making contracts, surveying the market and advertising.

Any staff employed should not have decision making autonomy or carry out normal management operations.

SET UP COSTS AND FORMALITIES

The French government has been accused of not making it easy for foreigners to set up a business in France. Since 1 January 1992 however, the procedure has been simplified. In theory at least the UK businessman should have no more problems than his French counterpart.

Registration

You are required to register the new business at the *Registre du Commerce* within two weeks of starting to trade. You will require:

- ◆ A company statute. This defines the business in terms of its legal structure, share capital, trading address and activity.

- ◆ Proof that share capital has been paid to a *notaire* or deposited in a bank.

- ◆ Documents of incorporation. These are sent to an administrative department – the *Centre de Formalities des Enterprises* – and to the commercial court (*Greffe du Tribunal du Commerce* which in turn inform the tax and social security departments that you are in business.

- ◆ A notice of incorporation for publication in a legal register – the *Bulletin of Civil and Commercial Properties*.

- ◆ Standard form notices for local newspapers.

- ◆ An application to register with the *Repertoire des Metiers* (trade register), the *Chambre de Commerce et l'Industrie* (chamber of commerce and industry), and possibly with local trade associations.

Professional advice

Theoretically you can deal with all these matters yourself. It is recommended though that you take professional advice. French bureaucracy is not noted for encouraging individualism. Many of these documents have to be prepared

in a precise form, and will be returned if they are incomplete
or imprecise.

Registration fees

These are both fixed and flexible charges. According to one
trade survey the average cost of completing a business set up
in 2002 was just under €1,300.

A typical breakdown would be:

Registering a limited company	€200
Tax on authorised share capital outlay	€65
Incorporation fees for a limited company	€500
Legal announcements and print costs	€170
Additional professional services	€400
Total	€1,335

BUYING A COMMERCIAL PROPERTY

Fonds de commerce

The legal process for buying business premises is similar to
that for the purchase of domestic property.

However, there is one important difference. In French law
the property is a separate entity to the business itself. The
business – the *fonds de commerce* includes the trading name,
licences, vehicles, fixtures and fittings, stock, and intangible
assets that include goodwill.

The *fonds de commerce* is, in effect, a separate contract. The business can sometimes be sold, or reassigned, without the property itself changing hands.

The preliminary contract

The contract for the purchase of commercial property includes the following elements:

◆ Agreed price and method of payment.

◆ A deposit – normally 10% of the agreed price – which is held by the selling agent or *notaire*.

◆ The legal identification of the property itself and the vendors and purchasers.

◆ A description of any additional rights or restrictions that apply to the property.

◆ The vendor's declaration that the property is sold with vacant possession.

◆ An agreed date for completion.

◆ Any special conditions (*clauses suspensives*) that will terminate the transaction. One such condition may be that the deal is subject to the buyer raising a loan or mortgage. As with domestic property this protects the deposit if the deal cannot be financed.

LEASING COMMERCIAL PROPERTY

Almost half of commercial property in France is leased. Leases are for a minimum of nine years unless a shorter period is agreed in advance by both parties.

As with domestic property the commercial lease is weighed heavily in favour of the tenant, and the formal documents are very similar.

Renewing the lease

Although the business is separate from the building, it is recognised that in practice the two are interdependent. The tenant therefore has the right to renew the lease by informing the landlord of his intention to continue trading. This must be done, in writing, six months before the lease expires.

Rent

This is negotiable and becomes part of the formal agreement. Sometimes the amount payable is linked to an agreed index, with the provision that any rise or fall of more than 25% will be subject to an independent review. This would take into account market trends, property values and base rates.

If the rent is not indexed the landlord is allowed to change (which invariably means increase) the rent every three years. These increases may not be more than the standard index of housing construction during the three year period. The only exception to this is if the premises have been improved at the landlord's expense and this must add more than ten per cent to the property's market value. Even in these circumstances the law provides strict limits on how much more the landlord can charge.

Hotels and certain kinds of office properties are subject to slightly different rules. In some cases rent increases may be related to business turnover. This is similar to the situation in which the tenant of a UK public house can find himself. Successful trading sometimes appears to be 'punished' by a substantial rent increase. In France increases have to be justified.

The responsibilities of the tenant

Again these are very similar to those applied to a domestic lease. Basically the tenant is responsible for regular payment of rent and the other charges on the property.

Contact clauses may limit the kind of business activity he may carry out from a particular property. The landlord's approval must also be sought for a change of trading activity, or any sub-letting of the property.

The landlord can also insist that any activity is formally registered with the appropriate trades organisation and subject to their rules. These restrictions are necessary because tenants of commercial property often transfer responsibility for the lease from themselves to their business. This, in turn, could be either sold or reassigned.

Droit au bail

A deposit – the *droit au bail* is required at the time the lease is signed. This is normally the equivalent of three or six months advance rental. The amount is normally returnable at the end of the lease period.

Eviction compensation

If the tenant has fulfilled his obligations, and the renewal of a lease is refused, he is entitled to compensation. Again there is a complex formula which takes into account the value of the business, the cost of relocation and resettling, and any additional staff travel costs.

In practice eviction compensation is not something that many landlords would contemplate. They are more likely to find a pretext, such as a change in trading activity made without the landlord's approval.

FINANCING A BUSINESS

The business plan

French banks may be approached with a business plan. This should be prepared to a professional standard and drafted in French.

It will include:

◆ A market evaluation.

◆ A full description of the intended operation.

◆ Details of intended capital purchases, including property and leases.

◆ The intended legal format and constitution of the company.

◆ Cash flow forecasts.

◆ A full asset and investment profile.

◆ A forecast of accounts for the first three years of trading.

For anything more than the most modest business venture, this information should be compiled by an accountant (*un comptable*) or a professional auditor (*commissaire au comptes*).

Loans

Finance is generally raised from one of three sources:

A UK bank

A UK bank will approach the matter in much the same way as they would for the setting up of a UK business, but is likely to require additional security and safeguards.

The Venture capital sector

One way in which French companies raise money is through the circulation of a promotional prospectus on the capital markets. This accounts for around 40% of credit and short-term finance. Rates of interest are very competitive.

A French bank

French banks offer a number of arrangements. The principal forms of finance generally amount to loans or leasing contracts for between two and 20 years. Loans are normally available for up to 80% of the total investment subject to depreciation of stock and equipment.

When the business involves a property purchase, even where this is domestic premises used as a small business base, the loan will invariably be secured against the property.

Finance of 100% is sometimes available for leasing arrangements. In this case a leasing company owns the premises for the duration of the lease, but the tenant has the right to buy when the lease contract is terminated.

French banks will normally require the following guarantees:

- A charge on the business.

- A mortgage on the property.

- A charge on certain items of equipment.

- An inventory of possessions.

- Insurance cover assigned to the bank.

Cheaper loans

Loans for smaller amounts, which must also not add up to more than 50% of the business, can sometimes be obtained on preferential rates from trade organisations.

Another form of loan is possible if you join a franchise network. In this case a bank will accept guarantees from a mutual guarantee society set up on behalf of the franchise operators. In some cases it is possible to obtain a loan that includes the cost of joining the network.

Traditionally interest rates in France have been lower than in the UK although more recently the difference has eroded considerably.

Tax breaks and incentives

The French government is keen to encourage employment and support investment in the country.

This means:

◆ Government subsidised loans are available to certain kinds of craftsmen and traders.

◆ Industrial business grants and subsidies are available on a regional basis. This is similar to the regional aid programme operating in the UK. It is EU funded and intended to help commercial and industrial regeneration. Information is available from the *conseil regional* in each area.

◆ Indirect grant aid is available in the form of tax abatement for new businesses. A 100% abatement on profit taxation applies for the first two years. This is followed by a sliding scale that reduces to a 25% abatement in the fifth year. Independent professionals and those selling financial services and insurance do not enjoy this abatement.

◆ *Taxes professionelles* are not levied in the first year. These are similar to the old UK rates system. The charge is based on a notional rental value of the property and assets. The bill can vary considerably according to location and exemptions beyond the first year are also determined on a local basis.

◆ Up to 25% of the initial investment in a business can be offset against personal income tax. The ceiling here is €1,500 for a single person and €3,000 for a married couple.

EMPLOYING OTHERS

Permits

Traditionally all those who worked in France required a work permit (*carte de travail*) and residence permit (*carte de séjour*).

This now only applies to non EU personnel. Members of the EU are given renewable five-year residence permits, but these still require full documentation.

Working hours

This has been defined since 1982 as:

◆ A standard 35-hour working week. Overtime is non-mandatory and must be paid at enhanced rates.

◆ Employees cannot be required to work on Sundays.

◆ A minimum paid holiday allowance of five weeks plus the 11 national holidays.

◆ Part-time contracts are notionally pro-rated. In practice this is difficult to administer and enforce. Most French people take their holidays in August, and most businesses are also closed on bank holidays. For all practical purposes most commercial activity grinds to a halt for seven weeks each year.

Wages

France has minimum wage legislation. However, this has been largely unenforceable since France began to suffer a significant employment problem a few years ago.

Theoretically the legal minimum wage is linked to the cost of living index.

◆ In September 2002 the legal minimum was €5.59 an hour.

◆ Semi-skilled workers normally receive a minimum wage 15 to 20% higher than the legal minimum. Skilled workers receive 40 to 50% more.

◆ Management salaries are generally within the range of €3,000 to €7,500 a month.

◆ Special conditions apply to those working in the hotel and catering sectors.

Contracts of employment
Anyone employed in France is entitled to a written contract.

This covers three main areas:

◆ The job description.

◆ The wage agreed.

◆ The legal position of the employee in terms of responsibilities within the company.

The contract can be for a fixed or indefinite period. Any contract that does not state the fixed period of employment is deemed to be indefinite.

Stringent warnings and procedures have to be followed before an employee can be dismissed from an indefinite contract. This is intended to prevent arbitrary dismissals.

The only genuine reasons accepted are proven criminality, misconduct or professional inadequacy.

Disputed cases are judged by a tribunal. Wrongful dismissal invariably brings a substantial entitlement to compensation. Fixed contracts must not be for longer than two years. Unless the employer can prove just cause for an earlier termination, the employee will receive a compensation sum at least equal to the remaining portion of his contract.

Welfare payments

Foreign companies with a base in France have to contribute to employment, health and retirement schemes on behalf of their employees. Those in employment also make their own contributions.

The only exception to this is in the case of temporary employment from other EU countries.

Contributions by, and on behalf of part-time workers are pro-rated according to the hours actually worked. In practice this is usually worked out as a propotion of income during a 'standard' month.

Contributions to the French welfare system have been traditionally higher than in the UK.

Recently the principal elements were:

| | Contribution percentage | | Earnings ceiling |
	Employer	Employee	
Sickness, maternity and disability	12.6	5.9	Full amount
State pension	8.2	7.6	Up to €21,605 p.a.
Widow's insurance	Nil	0.1	Full amount
Family allowance	7.0	Nil	Full amount

COMMUNICATIONS

Online services such as telephone, fax, and the internet are readily available.

Transmission

French communiction systems are as technically advanced as those in the UK but the failure rate is rather higher. The problem is that demand has constantly exceeded the number of lines, frequencies and channels available. During the CB boom of the 1970s, for instance, it became virtually impossible in some areas for the police to use their own equipment.

Computers

Computers are engineered to international standards, but configured for country of sale.

◆ French keyboards do not use the familiar QWERTY format. Software is written to take account of this.

◆ French keyboards and printers are configured slightly differently – to accept, for instance, the € sign rather than the £. More modern UK keyboards are configured for the euro, which is marked alongside number 4. In popular software packages, such as *Microsoft Office* or *Corel* press Alt Gr and 4. Alternatively go to 'Insert Symbol' to find €, which can then be configured for regular use as a 'shortcut'.

◆ A UK standard television cannot be used as a VDU. The PAL and Secam systems are incompatible. This will not affect PC users but it means that popular games consoles may not function without a compatible monitor.

Fax and modem

These will operate exactly the same way as in the UK. Note, however, that your modem will need a different connection to the telephone socket.

SETTING UP THE BUSINESS IN THE HOME

Domestic and commercial property

The situation is very similar to that found in the UK. Often it is a fine line that distinguishes domestic from business premises, but the judgements are usually based on the property itself and where it is situated.

A general rule is that each building is liable for rates either as domestic or commercial premises. The fact that your home may also be your registered office does not mean that the premises themselves are commercial. That is determined by the scale and type of activity carried on there.

In certain circumstances part of a domestic property could become liable for *taxes professionelles* – business rates. This would apply typically perhaps to a doctor or architect when part of his domestic premises are set aside and equipped exclusively for business use. Where this happens the property is divided for tax purposes into domestic and commercial sectors.

Another complexity arises from the fact that if you have a business in France you must also have a registered office. This, however, is not necessarily either your home or business premises. For the first two years, for instance, you can legally register your business at the office of your *notaire*.

Business and domestic loans

As in the UK there are loans for different purposes. A self-employed writer, artist or craftsman working from home can apply for a domestic mortgage. The bank would understand that the nature of this profession meant that an area may be set aside as an office or studio.

Future development

This has been described as 'a canvas of grey areas'. Adding an extra room, for instance, would probably not affect the tax, rates or loan situation. The assumption would be that the property was still primarily residential. Plans to build a studio that is wholly separated from the house could be interpreted differently.

The local town hall and chamber of commerce can advise in each case. Your business will already be registered with them and it is usually possible to get a quick ruling.

Other checks and safeguards

If you intend to work from home you should also make sure:

◆ That you have obtained your *carte de séjour* from the local *prefecture de police*.

◆ That your notaire is informed at the time of the property purchase that you intend to run a business from home. This will ensure that the terms of your freehold or lease do not exclude business activities. This is rarely a problem – unless the property is held under one of the formats of co-ownership.

◆ That your type of business can legally be run from home. Local trade associations and the chamber of commerce can offer advice here. In the larger cities bylaws forbid particular forms of business on domestic premises. Generally, however, the French tradition of personal liberty is upheld, but you would be unwise to think this extended to noisy nightshifts in a workshop in the middle of a housing estate.

◆ That your insurance cover is extended to business usage and, in certain cases, public liability.

10

Business taxation and insurance in France

THE AUDIT

With very few exceptions businesses registered on French soil must present an annual audited statement to the local commercial court.

The requirements are:

♦ A detailed balance sheet. This lists fixed assets, current assets and pre-paid expenses. Loss provision, accounts due, accrued expenses and deferred credits appear on the debit side.

♦ A statement of income. This details expenses and revenues that come from trading and financial transactions.

◆ An auditor's statement. This includes familiar phrases about 'the true and fair view' of the business's financial situation.

All registered companies are required by law to appoint an approved statutory auditor. He has to be independent of the client company and may not be involved in preparing the financial statements on which he reports. Auditors are normally appointed for a six-year term.

The following organisations can offer help with detailed enquiries:

Société Accredité de Representation Francais
2 Rue des Petits Peres
75002 Paris

INITIAL TAX LIABILITY

Initial tax liability depends on whether you are starting a new business or taking over an existing one.

Starting a new business normally involves the purchase of a *fonds de commerce*. The transfer duties apply to all assets transferred apart from goods subject to VAT (TVA).

The existing scale of charges is:

TRANSFER DUTY (Droits d'enregistrement)

Property value tax	National	Department	Local	Total
Less than €15,250	Nil	Nil	Nil	Nil
From €15,251 to €45,750	6%	0.6%	0.4%	7%
Value in excess of €45,751	11.8%	1.4%	1%	14.2%

In the case of a business takeover there is a one-off transfer duty charge of 4.8%. If, however, the new company is formed as a Société Anonyme (one form of limited company) there is no duty payable – as long as the legal transfer took place outside France.

Capital gains tax is not applied to business purchases.

BUSINESS LICENCE TAX (Taxe professionnelle)

In many ways this is similar to the business rate system formerly applied in the UK.

It is based on an agreed rental value of fixed assets. This includes a notional market value of a rented property. A distinctly French feature of the tax is that the fixed assets figure is taken to include 18% of salaries paid in the tax year before last.

The tax is abated in the first year, then generally on a sliding scale for up to five years.

The amount levied can vary enormously in percentge terms according to local incentives given to attract business. To complicate matters further *taxe professionelle* is a political hot potato. The policy, and therefore the amount charged, can change considerably following each round of local government elections.

Recently the lowest rate of *taxe professionnelle* levied in France was 11%. The highest was 26% and the median national average was 17.14%.

A typical small business bill may work out like this:

Value of property	€100,000
Value of additional fixed assets	€25,000
18% of payroll	€12,500
Total charge value	€137,500
Total tax payable at national median rate	€23,567

CAPITAL GAINS TAX (Taxe sur les plus values)

This is divided into short- and long-term gains. Short term is defined by assets held for less than two years. It also includes a portion of the revaluation of depreciable fixed assets held for less than two years.

Long-term gains are the sale of assets held for more than two years.

The rates applied are:

◆ For short-term gains – 39%.

◆ For long-term gains – 25% for land assets and 19% for fixed assets. If a company is subject to corporation tax this last figure is reduced to 16%.

CORPORATION TAX (Impôts sur les Sociétiés)

All businesses are registered in France subject to corporation tax apart from:

◆ New businesses, which are exempt for three years.

◆ Certain small businesses eligible for taxation under the simplified Business Income scheme.

The tax is currently 42% of distributed profits, and 39% of undistributed profits. It is collected quarterly.

The definition of taxable profit is similar to the formula applied in the UK. The main elements are:

◆ The difference between the cost value of stock at the beginning and end of the year. Added to this is the value of services, subsidies and income from fringe profits such as interest payments.

◆ Allowable expenses to set against this include the cost of salaries, welfare payments, interest on loans, depreciation of equipment, education and training expenses, and the purchase of certain goods.

TAXATION OF BUSINESS INCOME (Impôt sur les benefices industrielles et commerciaux)

This is the small business alternative to corporation tax. The definition of a small business can be complex, but it is normally taken to include:

◆ Sole traders.

◆ A partnership based on a limited liability company.

◆ A family owned limited liability company.

Businesses that qualify have profits taxed on a basis very similar to personal income tax although taxable profits are calculated as for corporation tax.

The Taxation of Business Income scheme has advantages when the chargeable rate of income tax is lower than corporation tax. This applies to most small businesses. In exceptional circumstances, however, it may be advantageous to change the legal identity of the business in order to fall into the net of corporation tax.

WAGES TAX (taxes sure les salaires)

This is regarded as a claw-back tax – rather similar to Class 4 National Insurance in the UK. It is applied only to businesses not required to register for VAT.

In 2002 the following rates were applied:

Company wage bill	Percentage charge
Nil – €5,700	4.25
€5,701 – €11,075	8.50
€11,076 – upwards	9.50

VALUE ADDED TAX (taxe sur la valeur ajoutée)

All business opertions in France are theoretically liable for VAT as long as an 'economic activity' is involved. This of course creates any number of grey areas. A Bureau de liaison (a 'Shop Window') does not always have to register. A branch or subsidiary office invariably does.

The French system is similar to that applied in the UK. However, there are no thresholds for registration. The requirement to register depends on the nature of business activity involved:

◆ Those involved in agricultural, trading, manufacturing and service industries are required to register.

◆ Salaried activities are normally exempt, as are insurance and medical activities, educational services and transactions subject to other taxes.

◆ Special rules apply to advertising, staffing agencies, research and the hire of equipment and machinery.

VAT is assessed on value added at each stage of production. A credit system is applied through which VAT is charged down the chain of production to point of sale. At this stage the bill is finally paid by the customer.

The assessment applies to all amounts received by sellers and suppliers in exchange for the services received or goods sold. In the case of product liability it is incurred at the time the goods are delivered. Services can be paid on an accruals basis.

VAT payable is calculated by deducting input from output VAT. Any excess paid will be refunded.

Form CA3

The standard VAT form (CA3) must be completed quarterly by small businesses. These are defined as companies that do not pay capital gains tax. Other businesses must make a monthly return.

VAT rates

The rates in force recently were:

Food, pharmaceuticals and water	0.5%
Cars, furs, perfumes and various luxury items	22%
Standard rate for most other items	18.6%
Some services	20.6%

Imported goods are subject to VAT in accordance with these rates.

BRANCH PROFITS TAX

The general rule is that all businesses conducted on French

soil are taxed as French companies. In certain circumstances, however, the branch may qualify to pay an additional branch profits tax. In practice reciprocal tax treaties mean that this can generally be avoided.

SUPPLEMENTARY FLAT RATE TAXATION

There are three minor areas of taxation applied to certain businesses with ten or more employees. In each case the tax is levied as a percentage of the wage bill.

Construction tax (participation construction)	0.65%
Training tax (participation formation continue)	1.20%
Apprentice tax (taxe apprentissage)	0.60%

Car tax

Tax on company vehicle ownership depends on the horse-power of the vehicle.

Ile de France

An additional annual levy is charged on the prime commercial sites in the Ile de France. This varies between €3 and €10 per square metre of surface area.

BUSINESS INSURANCE

Premium taxes

Insurance premiums are subject to tax at the following rates:

Motor vehicles	34.9%
Fire and combined policies	7% to 30%
Health policies	9%

Premium costs

These have been traditionally comparable with the UK. Also comparable is the way that premiums in certain areas, and for certain risks, have rocketed in recent years.

Documentation format

All French insurance policies follow a format prescribed by law:

◆ The risks and exclusions must be fully described.

◆ The level of cover and the obligations of both insurer and insured must be identified.

◆ The schedule describes matters that relate to the issue of the policy. These include registered addresses, the premium paid and renewal dates.

Renewals

French policies are automatically renewed unless written notice is given at least two months before the renewal date.

Claims

All claims must be notified within five working days of the insurable event. This is reduced to 24 hours in the case of theft.

Business cover

All registered businesses are expected to have the following insurance cover:

◆ Motor insurances for vehicles owned by the company.

◆ Health insurance – the *assurance complementaire maladie* – ensures the availability of health service facilities for all employees.

◆ Business property insurance against fire, theft, storm and water damage, and the breakage of glass.

Additional cover

Standard business cover is regarded as a legal minium.

Many companies also pay premiums for:

◆ Pensions and savings schemes.

◆ Accident and death at work.

◆ Consequential loss following fire, flood or other 'natural' event.

◆ Legal liabilites as the owner or tenant of a building.

◆ Transport of goods.

Job related cover

Certain types of enterprises require additional insurance cover. Architects, lawyers, and doctors require professional indemnity insurance. Cafes, hotels, restaurants and garages require public liability insurance.

The list is almost endless, and this fact alone begins to explain why the French insurance market is the fifth largest in the world.

11

The internet

For those who have access to it, the internet is the quickest way of obtaining information. From your home, you can book and pay for your holidays, or check on the climate and current weather for almost anywhere in the world.

BUYING A PROPERTY

There are many internet sites devoted to selling property in France. The following were amongst the longest established:

www.green-acre.com

This company not only lists available property, but if you register with them (free of charge) it will search for a property in the area/price range you designate. It has versions in both French and English and can act as an estate agent for you if you wish to sell your property.

www.french-property.com

A number of French estate agents use this site to advertise those properties they think will be attractive to UK buyers. This site has possibly the most properties for sale and at prices to suit all pockets. It will also put you in touch with other people looking for property so you can exchange ideas, etc. and you can buy books like this one through their bookshop.

www.french-property-news.com

A visit to this single site would permit you to find the property you wish to buy, be escorted to visit it, act as your agent during the purchase process, connect you to a mortgage broker, get a company to renovate it, another to act as agents for your gîte, obtain the services of a gardener and then sell it for you if you get tired of it. They offer advice on their Legal Tips page and will send you a regular newsletter.

www.frenchproperty.co.uk

Upmarket properties for sale, including small estates and holiday rentals.

www.coast-country.com

The English Estate Agents on the French Riviera have properties for sale and rent and links to sites offering weather forecasts and Riviera news.

www.timeshare-traders.com

Timeshare specialists.

www.abimmo.com

A French language site. You need to know the department number of your desired area to begin the search. The site is well signposted and easy to navigate after that.

www.123voyage.com

A site with links to many different aspects searching for a property in the right place.

www.abelcom.net

Lots of background information on France and your chosen region. Offers properties on a number of prinicipal rooms basis.

RENTING A PROPERTY

You may already be familiar with sites where individual owners advertise their property for short-term rental. These sites feature most frequently in internet searches:

www.cheznous.com

A comprehensive service offering properties from in-dividuals together with travel arrangements, holiday insurance and booking hotels en route to your destination.

www.gites-in-france.co.uk

Concerned mainly with *gîtes* for rental or sale.

www.webconnection.co.uk

Holiday rental, but with the addition of offering long winter lets ideal for those who wish to check out their location before buying.

www.frenchconnections.co.uk
Self catering gîtes and B&B.

www.ghestates.co.uk.
Offers luxury and secluded holiday accommodation in Charente and Dordogne.

www.chez-oz.com.au
Dont be put off by the title! Its run by an Australian company and has a wide range of gîtes on offer.

www.propertyinfrance.com
Opening page shows a number of properties for rent in each region. There are properties in all market sectors.

FINANCING THE DEAL

French and UK banks have already been mentioned. The following website can give you an immediate response, at least in principle: www.french-mortgage-connection.co.uk

MANAGING YOUR MONEY

Many UK banks have accounts which can be managed via the internet, but beware the bank that wants to charge you for the software to do it. There are also specialist internet banks.

Cahoot.com is an offshoot of HBSC and offers simple current accounts. www.egg.com is an offshoot of The Prudential which offers reasonably high interest rates on savings. www.virginone.com is part of the Royal Bank of

Scotland and offers special mortgage/current accounts for those whose salary is paid directly into the account.

Paying the bills

Income tax

The Inland Revenue permits you to fill in your tax return online and send it to them electronically. Their website is: www.inlandrevenue.gov.uk

This site has not always received the best press, especially from those filling in their returns at the last minute.

Standard UK bills

Girobank has a special site for paying bills on UK utilities: www.billspayment.co.uk

SHOPPING

For those who get easily homesick for British products, there are a number of UK high street stores that have a presence on the internet.

www.whsmith.co.uk – the well known book store.
www.blacks.co.uk – for all your camping/outdoor clothing
    needs.
www.debenhams.com – well known department store.

There are also specialist stores which can frequently though not always undercut the high street stores.

www.electricalwarehouse.co.uk – claims up to 60% off high street prices.

www.amazon.co.uk – books and music.

NEWSPAPERS

Many national and regional newspapers daily and weekly have internet sites to help keep you in touch.

www.sundaytimes.co.uk
www.guardian.co.uk

The Guardian will email you free of charge its daily, irreverent look at football. This is called, The Fiver. You can subscribe (free) by sending an empty email, with subscribe as the subject to:

fiver-request@footballunlimited.co.uk, or view the contents at www.footballunlimited.co.uk

RADIO

All the BBC radiobroadcasts can be received via www.bbc.co.uk

Further reading

Bed and Breakfast of Character and Charm in France (Fodor's Rivages)

Buying and Renovating Property in France, J. Kater Pollock (Flowerpoll)

Buying and Restoring Old Property in France, David Everett (Robert Hale)

Buying and Selling Residential Property in France (Chamber of Commerce)

Can We Afford the Bidet? Elizabeth Morgan (Lennard)

French Dirt, Richard Goodman (Pavilion Books)

French or Foe, Polly Platt (Culture Crossings)

French Law for Property Buyers, Kerry Schrader (French Property News)

Gîtes de France Official Handbook (Gîtes de France)

Home and Dry in France, George East (La Puce Publications)

The Legal Beagle Goes to France, Bill Thomas (Quiller Press)

Live and Work in France, Nicole Prevost Logan (How To Books)

Living as a British Expatriate in France (Chamber of Commerce)

Maison Therapy, Alaistair Simpson (New Horizon)

Setting Up a Small Business in France (Chambre of Commerce)

Some of My Best Friends are French, Colin Corder (Shelf Publishing)

Traditional Villages of Rural France, Bill Laws (BCA)

Understanding France, John P. Harris (Papermac)

ENGLISH LANGUAGE NEWSPAPERS AND MAGAZINES

Blue Coast, 32 rue Marechal Joffre, 06000, Nice

Boulevard, Madiatime France SA, 68 Rue des Archives, 75003 Paris

France Magazine, Dormer House, Stow-on-the-Wold, Glos. GL54 1BN

French Property News, 2A Lampton Road, London SW20 0LR

Focus on France, Outbound Publishing, I Commercial Rd., Eastbourne BN21 3XQ

Living France, 79 High St., Olney MK46 4EF

The Riviera Reporter, 56 Chemin de Provence, 06250 Mougins

Standard Long-Term Letting Contract

CONTRACT DE LOCATION
Loi No. 89–462 du 6 juillet 1989
LOCAUX VACANTS NON MEUBLES

Entre les soussignes (*between the signatories*)
BAILLEUR (*Property Owner*) ....
MANDATAIRE (*Agent/Valuer*) ....
Et LOCATAIRES (*Tenants*) ....
Le bailleur loue les locaux et equipements ci-apres designes au locataire qui les accept aux conditions suivantes. (*The owner rents the premises and equipment designated hereafter to the tenant who accepts them subject to the following conditions.*)

LOCAUX (*Premises*)..

. . . Habitation principale
. . . Professionel et Habitational principale
. . . Appartement   . . . Maison individuelle

DESIGNATION DES LOCAUX ET EQUIPMENTS PRIVATIFS

....

Garage No . . .   Place de station No . . .
Cave No . . .   Autre

(*private equipment and facilities*) . . .

ENUMERATION DES PARTIES ET EQUIPEMENTS COMMUNS

. . . Gardiennage   . . . Vide-ordures
. . . Interphone   . . . Ascenseur
. . . Antenne TV collect   . . . Chauffage collectif
. . . Eau chaude collective . . . Espace(s) vert(s)

(*shared equipment and facilities*)

FIXATION DU LOYER
(There follows a series of legal definitions of the property and its state of repair according to articles 17, 17B and 18 of the law. If in any doubt, consult your solicitor)

DURÉE INITIALE DU CONTRACT
(*Initial period of contract*) ....

RAISONS PROFESSIONALLES OU FAMILIALES DU BAILLEUR
(*Professional or family reasons for contract being less than three years*)

....

....

DATE DE PRISE D'EFFECT
(*Date contract comes into effect*)

....

MONTANTS DES PAIEMENTS
(*total amount of payments*)

Loyer mensuel (*monthly rent*)   ....
Taxes (*taxes*)   ....

Provisions sur charges (*provision for charges*)   ....

Total mensuel (*monthly total*)   ....

TERMES DE PAIEMENT (*Payment terms*)

Cette some sera payable d'advance et en totalite le . . . de chaque mois.
(*This sum will be payable in full and in advance on the . . . of each month.*)

REVISION DE LOYER (*rent review*)

Le loyer sera revisée chaque année le...............
(*The rent review takes place each year in ....*)

DEPÔT DE GARANTIE (*deposit*).................................

CLAUSE PARTICULIERE (*special clause*)......................

....

HONORAIRES À PARTAGER PAR MOITIE
(*Fees to be equally divided*)

HONORAIRES DE TRANSACTION (*transaction fees*) .....
HONORAIRES DE REDACTION (*drafting fees*) ....
FRAIS D'ETAT DES LIEUX (*local fees*) ....

DOCUMENTS ANNEXES (*appendices*)

These could include lists of locally defined charges, extracts from the regulations governing co-ownership, local regulations for the recovery of keys and references to neighbourhood rents.

CLES REMISES (*keys*)

Nombres de cles remises au locataire   ....
(*number of keys given to tenant*) ....

SIGNATURE DES PARTIES

Fait at signe a . . . le . . . en . . . originaux dont un remis a chacun des parties qui le reconnait.

.... LE BAILLEUR
.... LE(S) LOCATAIRE(S)
.... LA CAUTION

CONDITIONS GENERALES
A. CONTRAT D'UNE DURÉE MINIMALE DE
3 OU 6 ANS
(contract for a minimum of three or six years)

*RESILIATION – CONGE (*termination of lease*)

The TENANT must give a minimum of three months notice in writing. This can be reduced to one month in the case of loss of employment or poor health of a tenant over 60.

The OWNER must give a minimum of six months notice in writing. This can be reduced in the event that the tenant is not carrying out his obligations.

*RENOUVELLEMENT (*renewal*)

Six months before the end of the contract, the owner can propose renewal of contract in writing. Either: a) For less time, but a minimum of one year, under same conditions as previously. b) For a minimum of three or six further years under conditions to be agreed.

B. CONTRAT D'UNE DURÉE INFÈRIEURE DE 3 ANS
(*contract for less than three years*)

This contract is for a period of not less than one year and only comes into operation if the owner can prove family or professional reasons why it should be so. These reasons must be given on the contract.

CLAUSE PARTICULIÈRE CONCERNANT LES LOCAUX CONSTRUITS AVANT DE 1.9.1948
(clause only for properties constructed before 1.9.48)

This deals with the state of repair of the property and the minimum standards it must reach.

CHARGES

This clause permits the owner to recover from the tenant such charges as repairs to communal equipment, or taxes which correspond to services from which the tenant benefits. They are to be fixed annually.

The owner must provide the tenant with a complete breakdown of the charges at least one month before they are due.

DEPÔT DE GARANTIE (*deposit*)

The deposit may not exceed two months rent and it must be returned to the tenant not more than two months after the keys have been returned.

As in English law, it can be used to pay any debts left behind by the tenant, etc.

TRAVAUX EVENTUELS ENTRAINANT MODIFICATION DE LOYER

(*work which could lead to the modification of the rent*)
a) Work done by the tenant to ensure that the property remains up to minimum standards.
b) Improvements made by the owner.

OBLIGATIONS DU BAILLEUR

(*owners responsibilities*)
This includes such things as keeping the property in a good state of repair and keeping receipts for payments and charges.

OBLIGATIONS DU LOCATAIRE
(tenants responsibilities)
Including such things as making due payments, keeping the property in good order and permitting access by the owner or his appointed agent at an agreed time.

CLAUSE RESOLUTOIRE ET CLAUSE PENAL
(*penalty and termination clauses*)

The main termination clause permits the owner to terminate the contract after two months non-payment of rent.

The main penalty clause permits the owner to recover the cost of an expulsion order against the tenant.

SOLIDARITE INDIVISIBILITE – ELECTION DE DOMICILE
The contract is legally binding upon the heirs of either or both parties.

FRAIS – HONORAIRES (*Fees*)
All fees are joint responsibility.

Index

Advertising, 155
Agriculture, 9, 69
Apartments, 15, 37, 54, 63, 147, 149
Architects, 146, 194

Bailiff, 57
Bank accounts, 97, 99
Banking rules, 96
Building land, 137, 139, 143
Building permit, 142
Bureaucracy, 168

Capital gains tax, 13, 101, 108, 186, 187
Caretaker, 12
Cheques, 97, 98, 99, 101
Citizenship, 65, 103
Climate, 2, 3, 28, 31, 32, 33, 34, 36, 37, 152
Code Napoleon, 6
Community tax, 101, 107
Computers, 180
Condominiums, 15
Consulate, 66, 70, 93
Contracts, 59, 130, 132, 134, 141, 147, 148, 163, 165, 170, 174, 177, 178, 179
Conveyance, 132
Co-ownership, 114, 130, 148, 183, 206
Culture, 1, 29, 37

DATAR, 103
Death duties, 101
Dentist, 70, 72
Deposit, 131, 132, 148, 149, 170
Doctor, 70, 71, 73, 181, 194
Domicile, 102, 103, 108, 109, 113, 115, 121
Driving, 90
Driving licence, 90, 91

Education, 3, 12, 75, 104, 188, 190
Electricity, 54, 78, 80, 82, 139, 142, 157
Embassy, 77
Emigrating, 12
Estate agents, 13, 15, 16, 17, 126, 128, 129, 163

Fax, 181
Finance, 13, 119, 121, 174
FNAIM, 21, 24, 34
Formality, 138, 166

Garden, 16, 26, 139, 140
Gas, 82
Gift tax, 101, 111
Gîte, 22, 51, 52, 53, 54, 55, 62,
    102, 150, 153, 157, 159, 161,
    199
Grants, 76, 176

Health, 11, 12, 69, 72, 73, 122,
    179, 192, 194, 207
Holidays, 26, 28, 30, 36, 51, 177
Hotel, 51, 101, 111, 171, 178,
    194

Importing, 66, 92
Inheritance, 48, 59, 109, 110,
    111, 112, 113, 114, 118, 136
Insurance, 8, 12, 55, 59, 70, 73,
    74, 82, 90, 93, 94, 95, 121,
    122, 124, 126, 141, 153, 157,
    175, 176, 180, 183, 184, 190,
    192, 193, 194, 195, 198
Internet, 196, 199
Inventories, 155

Law, 6, 55, 56, 69, 76, 80, 90,
    98, 101, 103, 109, 112, 113,
    115, 116, 123, 124, 127, 132,
    134, 141, 146, 149, 153, 164,
    165, 166, 169, 171, 185, 208
Lawyer, 129
Lease, 55, 108, 124, 170, 171,
    172, 173, 174, 183
Letting, 52
Letting, long term, 55
Letting, short term, 10, 153

Medicines, 70, 71, 111
Mobile phones, 84
Mortgage, 12, 58, 119, 120, 121,
    124, 131, 149, 153, 159, 170,
    175, 182

Newspapers, 16, 52, 88, 156,
    168, 201, 203
Notaire, 109, 116, 118, 124,
    130, 132, 133, 134, 135, 139,
    143, 148, 153, 155, 159, 162,
    163, 168, 170, 182, 183

Penalty clauses, 56, 58, 131,
    141, 148

Radio, 87, 201
Removal, 66, 67
Renting, 10, 51

Schools, 75, 76, 77
Stamp duty, 135
Subsidies, 121, 176, 188
Survey, 13, 16, 144
Surveyors, 132, 146

Tax, 12, 55, 56, 67, 93, 97, 98, 101, 102, 103, 104, 105, 106, 107, 108, 109, 110, 111, 112, 116, 136, 152, 154, 157, 158, 159, 165, 167, 168, 175, 176, 182, 184, 185, 186, 188, 189, 191, 192, 200
Telephone, 83, 157, 180, 181
Television, 5, 81, 86, 181
Tenure, 57

Timeshare, 51, 59, 61, 67, 197
Tontine, 116
Tribunal, 7, 145, 168, 179
TVA, 111, 112, 127, 151, 152, 185, 190, 191

Visa, 64

Water, 54, 82, 139, 142, 191, 194
Will, 116